KNITTING SOCKS FROM AROUND THE WORLD

Kari Cornell, Editor

Photography by
Sue Flanders and Janine Kosel

Voyageur Press

First published in 2011 by Voyageur Press, an imprint of MBI Publishing Company, 400 First Avenue North, Suite 300, Minneapolis, MN 55401 USA

Voyageur Press titles are also available at discounts in bulk quantity for industrial or sales-promotional use. For details write to Special Sales Manager at MBI Publishing Company, 400 First Avenue North, Suite 300, Minneapolis, MN 55401 USA.

To find out more about our books, visit us online at www.voyageurpress.com.

ISBN-13: 978-0-7603-3969-5

Editor: Kari Cornell
Technical Editor: Charlotte Quiggle
Photography: Sue Flanders and Janine Kosel
Design Manager: LeAnn Kuhlmann

Library of Congress Cataloging-in-Publication Data

Knitting Socks from Around the World / Kari Cornell, Editor ; Photographs by Sue Flanders and Janine Kosel.
     pages cm
ISBN 978-0-7603-3969-5 (flexibound)
 1. Knitting--Patterns. 2. Socks. I. Cornell, Kari A., 1970- editor. II. Flanders, Sue, 1960- photographer. III. Kosel, Janine, 1964- photographer.
TT825.K648 2011
746.43'2--dc22
                        2010046570

Additional Photo Credits:
Page 13: A woman knits on a hillside near Hardanger, Norway, 1890s. Credit: Senator Knute Nelson Collection, Vesterheim Archive
Page 47: A vintage postcard a woman in Welsh costume, tending to her knitting. Credit: Voyageur Press Archive
Page 73: Children with their knitting, Leipzig, Germany, 1907. Credit: Voyageur Press Archive
Page 109: A young Japanese woman in traditional dress with knitting needles. Credit: Voyageur Press Archive
Page 141: American children knitting for the Red Cross. Credit: Library of Congress

ACKNOWLEDGMENTS

Without the help of the following talented people, this book would not have been possible: Thanks so much to the designers: Star Athena, Dawn Brocco, Beth Brown-Reinsel, Tatyana Chambers, Donna Druchunas, Teva Durham, Gretchen Funk, Chrissy Gardiner, Anne Carrol Gilmour, Wendy J. Johnson, Janel Laidman, Elanor Lynn, Hélène Magnússon, Annie Modesitt, Heather Ordover, Beth Parrott, Elizabeth Ravenwood, Kristin Spurkland, Candace Eisner Strick, Pinpilan Wangsai, and Anna Zilboorg, for providing such inspiring sock designs for this book. A special thank you to Nancy Bush for her lovely designs and thoughtful introduction. Many thanks to Charlotte Quiggle for her sharp technical edit and good humor. And I can't thank Sue Flanders and Janine Kosel enough . . . for their spot-on sense of styling, the countless hours they spent photographing the socks in just the right setting, and the many trips made to exchange socks with Charlotte.

Sue Flanders and Janine Kosel wish to extend a special thanks to the following photography sites:

Sibley House, www.mnhs.org/places/sites/shs
Minnesota Pioneer Park, http://pioneerpark.org
Eloise Butler Wild Flower Garden, http://eloisebutler.org/
Lyndale Peace Garden, www.minneapolisparks.org/

Thanks also to the following people who modeled socks: Terje Alming, Katie Day, Alice Flanders, LeAnn Kuhlmann, Nathan Meschke, Brooke Paynter, and Alison Michelle van Scheers.

CONTENTS

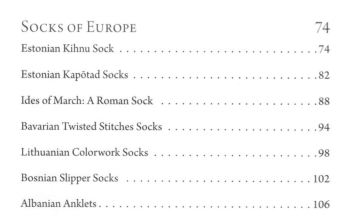

INTRODUCTION

By Nancy Bush

The first item of clothing identified as a sock was made from woven fabric, perhaps fulled, cut, and sewn together into a shape that would roughly fit a foot. Adjustments were made and eventually these items were shaped so that they fit as well as could be expected, considering that the woven material didn't have much stretch. To create some give in these stockings, the necessary shapes were cut along the grain of the woven fabric or on the bias (diagonally across the woven fabric). The seams, darts, and tucks used to shape the garment were soon hidden under decorative embellishments like embroidery, couching, and other fancy stitching.

The first socks made with yarn were not knitted, but looped, made in Egypt as early as the fourth century. The examples that exist today look like true knitting, with each stitch crossed or twisted. Upon close examination, it was discovered that these early socks were actually made with a looping technique that resembles knitting, except that the stitches won't unravel when cut.

In Viking times (roughly 790 to 1066 AD) and later, even into the twentieth century in some parts of northern Europe, foot coverings resembling socks or stockings were also made using a looping technique known as needle looping or *nålbinding* in Swedish. Textiles made in this technique are warm and offer superior protection from northern winter weather.

Both of these similar techniques require short lengths of yarn and a wooden, bone, or metal needle with an eye, similar to a bodkin or darning needle. Stitches are made by looping the working yarn through previously made loops. The process is slow and the result is rather course.

True or classic knitting is believed to have its origins in the Middle East, likely in Islamic Egypt. It is possible that knitting was a progression from the looping technique mentioned above, and may very well have been done with hooked needles. One of the oldest known pieces of true knitting was found in what is now Cairo. This fragment was part of a collection belonging to a Swiss textile expert, Fritz Iklé, who dated the piece from the seventh to ninth centuries. It has sadly been lost, but was documented, along

A Dutch girl knits socks in this charming vintage postcard.

with an image, in *Mary Thomas's Knitting Book* (1938). The knitted piece was made of silk, in crossed stockinette stitch (where each stitch is twisted) at a gauge of about 36 stitches (15 cm) to an inch. As this was a fragment, it is impossible to know what the original item was.

Chronologically, the next knitting that can be dated to sometime between the twelfth and fifteenth centuries are blue and white knitted stockings, examples of which are in the collection of the Textile Museum in Washington, D.C. These stockings, made of cotton in stockinette stitch, were knitted from the toe up. They and others like them, found in various museums, are thought to be the earliest known true knitted foot coverings. There also exist fragments of true knitting, with similar patterning, but it is unknown if they formed parts of stockings or other items, such as bags or perhaps hand coverings.

The craft of knitting is believed to have made its way into southern Europe by the thirteenth century. We have two knitted cushions as evidence of this, placed in Spanish tombs around 1275 AD. These pieces are some of the earliest examples of knitting known in Europe. The ornate two-color patterning and fine gauge (20 stitches to 1 inch) offer evidence that they were made by a highly skilled craftsperson. The fine metal needles necessary for such intricate work was evidence of the skill of Spanish-Arab metalworkers.

True knitting was also used in other textiles of the same period; knitted relic purses were made to hold saint's relics, and there are knitted gloves, worn by abbots and bishops for religious ceremonies, that date from the thirteenth century. The origin of these ancient textiles is unknown, so it is impossible to say with certainly that the craft of knitting was widespread throughout Europe. The fineness of the work could lead one to speculate that there were one or two highly skilled workshops operating at this early date, to supply knitted goods to specialized clients, such as the church.

KNITTING GAINS POPULARITY

It is only a short stretch of the imagination to realize that the wider population would adopt the same techniques used to knit these hand and foot coverings. The skill of knitting spread due to several factors: Knitting could be done with a few handmade tools. Yarn was readily available, and spindle spinning was a known skill. The techniques of knitting were not difficult to learn and, perhaps most importantly, knitted fabric could be made to fit special shapes, like feet and fingers. Stockings, gloves, and hats needed to fit close to the body, required stretch in order to be put on, and offered protection from the elements. Because knitting was done with long lengths of spun fiber, it was quicker and easier than nålbinding or needle looping and required fewer tools and less space than weaving. If a mistake was made, knitting was easily pulled out, while *nålbinding* or needle looping is almost impossible (or at best very slow) to pull out. For

all of these reasons, knitting must have been considered the "wonder textile" of its day, and as such, became very popular, very quickly.

THE EVOLUTION OF THE MODERN SOCK

Mentions of fine knitted stockings in Europe first appear in records from the mid 1500s, in accounts of clothing belonging to royalty and the more well-to-do in England. Henry VIII owned "six pairs of black silk hose knit" while his daughter Mary I had twenty-seven pairs of cloth hose supplied to her. She likely had access to knit silk hose from Spain, as she married Phillip II of Spain in 1554. By this time Spain was a known source of finely knit silk stockings, due in part to their ability to make fine-gauge steel knitting needles. Other records indicate that knitted hose made in England were becoming more common. In 1560 Elizabeth I was given a pair of silk stockings, knitted in England. She was so pleased with them that she declared she would never wear cloth stockings again, and after 1577 she was supplied with only knitted silk stockings. Knitting became a common activity during Elizabeth's reign (1558–1603).

The first worsted spun stockings were made in England around 1560. This was the beginning of England's great worsted industry, the foundation of much of the British Empire's wealth. These worsted stockings were finer than the coarser woolen spun stockings and could be compared to silk in comfort and delicacy. Both woolen and worsted stockings and socks were made by hand and worn by all classes of people. The making of these stockings also provided work for thousands of people, with buyers at home and abroad. Beginning in the 1600s, hand knitters competed with machine knitters to make enough stockings to keep up with the demand.

SOCK STYLES AROUND THE WORLD

Socks are one of the necessities of life for at least half of the world's population. Those who live in warm climates might not think of socks as necessary, but those who live in colder climates surely do. They offer protection, warmth, and at the end of the day, decoration. Among everyday folk in northern lands, socks and stockings were utilitarian and also offered a way to add color, pattern, and excitement to what might have been an otherwise drab existence. We can only speculate on the stockings women wore, as they were

Bosnian slipper socks, by Donna Druchunas

where seams used to be on cut and sewn hose. Fancy stitches down the ankle area of the sock, known as "clocks," offered an abundant canvas for the creative and inspired knitter. Both the Finnish Sock and the Estonian Kihnu Sock patterns feature clocks. Knitters added textured stitches, colored yarns, or embroidery for decoration on the finished sock, and even incorporated special symbols into the design to protect the wearer or bring them luck.

The many folk cultures found in northern Europe developed a variety of interesting clothing styles and unique patterns to decorate themselves. To my mind, some of the most interesting techniques, patterns, and cuts of clothing were created and worn by those living in cottages rather than castles. The wealth of patterns and skill found in the knitting alone is rich and varied. Studying the socks and stockings of the folk knitters of the past is a mirror into their history. One gets glimpses of places that were isolated, such as central Sweden, in the province of Dalarna, where the technique of *tvåändstickning* (two-end knitting) was strong. This technique, which is used in the Midsommer Blommer Socks pattern, didn't travel far from where it originated. One of the words in Swedish for this special technique translates to "doing it up like a sock," reflecting one of the main items of clothing that was made using the technique.

Stockings played a great role in Scotland, as seen in the tradition of kilt hose. Early Scots were known as "red shanks" for their lack of leg coverings, wearing only a plaid woven blanket, which became the kilt of modern times. When they began to cover their legs, they used cut and sewn plaid fabric that eventually became the knitted argyle patterning we know today. The kilt hose take the idea of stockings to be worn with a kilt into a more decorative area, with twining of cables and ornate texture.

While some patterns didn't travel far from where they were invented, others traveled the world, often with sailors as they fished for cod or delivered goods from port to port. It is likely that the X and O figures we think of as

almost always hidden under flowing skirts. Men's stockings, on the other hand, were much more visible, especially in the sixteenth century, due to the fashion of the time. These stockings showed fantastic decoration, and were colored, embroidered, and decorated to an extreme.

Small amounts of precious colored yarns could be used in decorating these smaller items of clothing, such as the Swedish Peerie socks or the Turkish socks. The surface could be covered in texture, such as the Gansy and Bavarian twisted-stitch socks, both decorated with ornate textured stitches. A lady could dress modestly, yet have a riot of color and ornate pattern hiding just above the ankle.

While everyone in northern climates needed socks and stockings, not all stockings were one and the same—the wearer's social class was reflected in these humble garments. The stockings of kings and queens were made of colored silk, and embroidery of gold thread covered the areas that were once decorated on the sewn hose of earlier times. Merchants and farmers, sailors and servants alike saw the finery of the upper classes, and these ideas became the fads and fashions of the times. Decorating stockings was just part of it. The ornate "seams" weren't really seams at all, but the memory of typical Fair Isle patterns were inspired by woven belts and knitted patterns from Baltic ports. Those designs probably made their way to the Shetland Islands on a fishing boat. Patterns were also introduced from one culture or tradition to another through marriage. Women often took family patterns and village ideas with them when they married into a family over the hill or across the sea—the Finnish socks are an example of this.

Many other ornate patterns found on knitted fabric are cross-cultural. A good example of this is the eight-pointed star, found on Turkish rugs and the Norwegian socks in this text. This pattern has traveled the world and, happily, suits knitting very well because it can be worked in a grid configuration. Other socks and stockings were made using the material at hand, one color of yarn, and simple stripes, or no pattern at all.

True knitting wasn't known in South America until the Spanish Conquest brought the skill to the indigenous people. With plenty of raw materials at hand, including alpaca and llama, they adapted knitting into their culture. Our Peruvian Socks are inspired by patterns from the region.

Construction of socks and stockings also varied from place to place. Most socks from northern Europe were made from the top down, while socks from the Balkans and further east, were typically made from the toe up. Examples of this type of construction can be seen in the Bosnian and Albanian Sock patterns.

In the Far East, knitted stockings were unknown until Europeans brought the skill of knitting with them. In Japan, socks made of cut and sewn cotton fabric with a separation for toes were worn with traditional sandals. The text offers a modern, knitted example of these traditional Japanese *tabi* socks.

In modern times, knitters continue to find inspiration in traditional techniques. Sock knitters are no longer knitting day and night to earn enough to pay the rent or to feed the family, nor are they reduced to using one type of yarn, spun at home in one or two colors. They have every choice imaginable, from spun by hand to mill-spun and imported from the other side of the world.

This collection of socks, inspired by traditions, places, and people from around the world, is a cross-section of the many possibilities there can be for knitting a sock. There is interesting "architecture," structure, and construction; varied, bold, and charming decoration; and glimpses into traditions that shaped the ideas behind the designs and patterns. We hope you enjoy this trip around the world in knitted socks!

Our collection of Favorite Socks from Around the World.

11

SOCKS OF SCANDINAVIA

Midsommar Blommor Socks

MIDSOMMAR BLOMMOR SOCKS

DESIGN BY W. J. JOHNSON OF SAGA HILL DESIGNS

This sock employs a knitting technique from my Swedish heritage. *Tvåändstickning* (two-ended knitting) is a double-knitting technique that creates a dense knitted fabric. It's ideal for garments that receive heavy wear, such as mittens and socks/slippers. For the two-color "cuff" pattern, I chose a traditional design from the Hälsingland province of Sweden, where my father's family resides, slightly modifying it to create a continuous design around the cuff.

The heel of the sock is a traditional Swedish "peasant" heel and not form-fitting like contemporary turned heels. This type of heel allows the sock to be easily repaired in the heel or toe, should it develop a hole.

The sock sample is knit in colors that are commonly found in traditional Swedish socks: a natural white and red.

Sizes

Sizes include extra ease and are not meant to be form-fitted. The sock is designed to fit more like a slipper.

Woman's small [US sizes 3–5] (medium [US sizes 6–9], large* [US sizes 9–12]). Instructions are given for smallest size, with larger sizes in parentheses. When only 1 number is given, it applies to all sizes.

*Note: *Will also fit Man's shoe size 10½–14.*

Finished Measurements

Circumference: 7¼ (9¼, 10¾)" [18.5 (23.5, 27.5)cm]

Length: As desired by knitter

Materials 1

◆ Saga Hill Designs *Handpainted Silk/Wool Blend* (fingering weight; 70% merino wool/30% silk): 450 (500, 550) yds [411 (457, 503)m] Natural (MC); 50 yds [46m] Falun Red (CC) *Kits or yarn for this sock are available at www.SagaHill.com*

◆ Size 2 [2.75mm] double-pointed needles (set of 5) or size needed to obtain gauge

◆ *Optional*: Size 0 or 1 [2 or 2.25mm] double-pointed needles (if necessary to obtain gauge in stranded St st)

◆ Tapestry needle

Gauge

40 sts and 40 rnds = 4" [10cm] in twined-knitting and 2-color stranded St st.

Adjust needle size as necessary to obtain correct gauge.

PATTERN NOTES

- These socks are made from the top down; they feature a peasant heel.

- Twine-knitted fabric does not cling to the leg as single-strand knitted fabric does; a braided tie is threaded through the top of the sock to help to keep the sock in place—this is a traditional feature of twined socks.

- All sections of the sock, with the exception of the colorwork, are worked using twined knitting techniques. For ease in reading the pattern, instructions are written as standard "knit" or "purl" or variations (such as decreases or increases), but are worked with two strands of yarn that alternate and twist around each other (see Sidebar).

- The color pattern is worked in standard stranded stockinette stitch and is not twined. You may need to use smaller needles for the colorwork section so that the gauge will match the twined-knitting gauge. Strand the yarn not in use loosely on the wrong side to maintain the fabric's elasticity; do not carry yarn not in use more than 5 stitches—weave it in as necessary.

- The sample socks show two options of twined patterning that form a border on either side of the color pattern: Border Version 1 has one twine-purled round; Border Version 2 has two rounds of alternating crook stitch (a patterning technique used in twined knitting); this pattern is usually called "Chain Path." Since Chain Path requires an odd number of stitches, the stitch count will be decreased by 1 stitch on the preceding round and increased by 1 stitch on the following round.

SPECIAL ABBREVIATIONS

N1, N2, N3, N4: Needle 1, needle 2, needle 3, needle 4. After heel is positioned, N1 and N2 hold sole sts and N3 and N4 hold instep sts.

STITCH PATTERN

Chain Path (twined over an odd number of sts)

Rnd 1: *K1, p1 (carrying strand on RS in front of knit st); rep from * around, ending k1.

Rnd 2: *P1 (carrying strand on RS in front of knit st), k1; rep from * around, ending p1.

I chose to use a "Falun" red (a red found in the Falun iron mines in Dalarna, Sweden, and a traditional Swedish house color). I hand-dyed the yarn from my Saga Hill Minnesota Series Dyes™.

The merino/silk blend is also a wonderful fiber combination for a bed sock because it is warm, wicks moisture, and is incredibly soft. The loose fit makes it especially comfortable. ✍

COLOR PATTERN

See Chart on page 19.

TWINED KNITTING TECHNIQUE

Twined knitting is worked with two ends of a ball of yarn, so it's necessary to work from a center-pull ball. Hold both strands of the working yarn (one from the ball center and one from the outside of the ball) in your working hand (left or right depending on your knitting style) and separate the strands with your index finger. Knit the first stitch with one of the strands. To knit the next stitch, pick up the other strand and wrap it clockwise over the first strand and knit the stitch. Then pick up the first strand again and wrap that clockwise around the strand just used for the second stitch and knit with that. Keep knitting by alternating strands in this manner. If you are knitting correctly, the back side of your work will have an even "twining" of stitches that run in the same horizontal direction.

Purled twined stitches are worked in the same manner by wrapping them clockwise around each other, but the yarns are held to the front of the work, as with a normal purl stitch.

INSTRUCTIONS

Make a slipknot with both ends of the MC ball (one from the inside of the ball, one from the outside) and put it on a dpn. Using long-tail method and both ends of MC, CO 72 (108, 108) sts (not counting the first slipknot). Remove the first slipknot and distribute the sts evenly onto 4 dpns with 18 (27, 27) sts on each dpn. Mark beg of rnd and join, taking care not to twist sts.

TIE CASING

Using twined technique knit 15 rnds. *If working Border Version 2, dec 1 on last rnd.*

LEG

Border Version 1

Rnd 1: Using twined method, purl around.

Border Version 2

Rnds 1 and 2: Work Chain Path pat on odd number of sts.

Continuing in twined knitting, knit 3 rnds. *Inc 1 on first rnd if you worked Border Version 2.* Cut 1 strand of MC.

Using smaller needles if necessary to maintain gauge, work 17 rnds in standard two-color stranded St st following chart.

Cut CC and re-join second strand of MC.

The sock will be worked only in twined knitting from this point to end.

Knit 3 rnds. *If working Border Version 2, dec 1 on last rnd.*

Rep 1st- or 2nd-round Border, working same version as before.

Small and large only

Knit 2 rnds. Inc 1 on first rnd if you worked Border Version 2.

Medium only

Knit 1 rnd. Do not inc 1 on this rnd if you worked Border Version 2.

Dec rnd: K3, [k2tog, k5] 14 times, k2tog, k3, k2tog—92 sts. If you worked Border Version 2, do not work last k2tog. Redistribute sts as necessary so that there are 23 sts on each dpn.

YARN MANAGEMENT

It's much easier to knit in the twined style if you put your ball into a "yarn bra," available at many yarn shops. You can also make your own from cut-up lengths of pantyhose.

If your working strands become twisted, put a needle through the ball of yarn (anchoring the yarn ends) and let the ball spin until the twist is undone.

Knit 4 rnds, ending last rnd on N3.

Prepare peasant heel position: Using 1 strand waste yarn and standard (non-twined) knitting method, knit across N4 and N1.

FOOT

Return to N4 and MC strands; mark new beg of rnd (N4 becomes N1, etc.) and continue around in twined knitting. Work even until foot measures approx 1½ (2, 2½)" [4 (5, 6.5) cm] short of desired length.

TOE

Rnd 1 (dec): N1: K1, k2tog, knit to end; N2: knit to last 3 sts, ssk, k1; N3 and N4: work as for N1 and N2—68 (88, 104) sts.

Rnd 2 (small and medium only): Knit.

Rep [Rnds 1 and 2 (Rnds 1 and 2, Rnd 1)] 7 (10, 14) times, ending with Rnd 1—40 (48, 48) sts with 10 (12, 12) sts on each dpn.

Transfer sts from N2 to N1 and sts from N3 to N4—20 (24, 24) sts on each dpn.

Cut both strands of yarn, leaving a 12" [30.5cm] tail for one strand (to be used for grafting) and a 6" [15cm] tail for the other; leave shorter tail on inside of sock to be woven in later.

With tapestry needle and longer tail, graft heel closed using Kitchener st.

PEASANT HEEL

Pick out waste yarn at heel, placing live sts on dpns as you go and fudging in the corners as necessary so that there are 18 (23, 27) sts on each dpn, with N1 starting in a corner—72 (92, 108) sts.

Knit 2 rnds.

Continue as for toe, finishing with Kitchener st.

BRAID

(Make 2)

Cut four 30" [76cm] lengths of MC and two 30" [76cm] lengths of CC. Hold strands together and double-knot 1 end, leaving 2" [5cm] at end for tassel. Separate the strands into 3 double-strand sets: 2 MC sets and one CC set. Work standard three-strand braid until about 3" [7.5cm] rem, tie ends into a double-knot. Trim the tassels to 1" [2.5cm]. *Note: If you don't have anyone to hold the end of your braid while you're working it, pin the end to a firm surface.*

FINISHING

Weave in all ends. Fold the top edge down for tie casing, laying the braid in the fold. Invisibly sew the top edge down to just above the border (making sure that you don't sew through the braid), leaving about 1″ [2.5 cm] at the center front for the braid ties to exit.

COLOR PATTERN

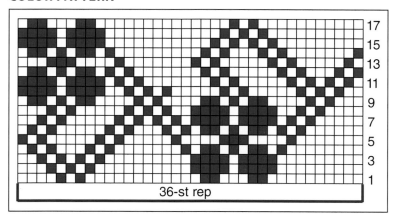

COLOR KEY
☐ MC
■ CC

RECOMMENDED RESOURCES

Twined Knitting: A Swedish Folkcraft Technique, by Ulla Danielsson. 1989, Interweave Press, Loveland, CO.

Two-Ended Knitting, by Anne-Maj Ling. 2004, Schoolhouse Press, Pittsville, WI.

BOHUS-STYLE PEERIE SOCKS

DESIGN BY DAWN BROCCO

These socks combine Swedish Bohus and Scottish Fair Isle traditions. The corrugated rib is an element in the traditional Fair Isle style, whereas the leg motifs are Fair Isle peerie patterns, but, by simply substituting certain stitches in purl, they become Bohus in style. Bohus-style knitting originated as a cottage industry in Sweden's Bohuslän province during World War II. Purl stitches worked into intricate colorwork patterns are a defining characteristic of Bohus designs, giving added dimension to the work. ❧

Sizes
Woman's small [US sizes 4–6] (medium [US sizes 6–9]; large [US sizes 8–11]). Instructions are given for smallest size, with larger sizes in parentheses. When only one number is given, it applies to all sizes.

Finished Measurements
Foot circumference: 7¼ (8, 8¾)" [18.5 (20.5, 22)cm]

Length from cuff top to lower heel: 7" [18cm]

Foot length: 9¼ (9¾, 10½)" [23.5 (25, 26.5)cm]

Materials 🔲4
◆ Cascade Yarns Cascade 220 (worsted weight; 100% Peruvian wool; 220 yds [201m] per 3½ oz [100g] skein): 1 (1, 2) skein(s) Sand #9499 (MC); 13 (15, 17) yds [12 (14, 18.5)m] Flamingo Pink #7805 (D)

◆ Cascade Yarns Cloud 9 (worsted weight; 50% merino/50% angora; approx 109 yd [99.5m] per 1¾ oz [50g] ball): 13 (15, 17) yds [12 (14, 18.5)m] each Purple #147 (A) and Copper Brown #134 (B); 7 (8, 9) yds [6.5 (7.5, 8)m] Natural #101 (C)

◆ Size 4 [3.5mm] double-pointed needles (set of 4) or size needed to obtain gauge

◆ Size 3 [3.25mm] double-pointed needles (set of 4)

◆ Tapestry needle

Gauge
24 sts and 32 rnds = 4" [10cm] in St st with larger needles.

24 sts and 28 rnds = 4" [10cm] over charted pat with larger needles.

Adjust needle size as necessary to obtain correct gauge.

PATTERN NOTES

◆ This sock is worked from the cuff to the toe. It has a flap heel, a V-heel turn, and a spiral toe.

◆ Carry stranded yarn loosely to maintain elasticity of sock.

◆ If using suggested yarn, gently hand-wash the socks to prevent felting.

SPECIAL ABBREVIATIONS

N1, N2, N3: Needle 1, needle 2, needle 3, with N1 and N3 holding gusset/sole sts and N2 holding instep sts.

INSTRUCTIONS

CUFF

With MC and larger dpns and using long-tail method, CO 44 (48, 52) sts in K1, P1 rib. Distribute sts evenly on 3 dpns; mark beg of rnd and join, taking care not to twist sts.

Rnd 1: [K1 A, p1 MC] around. Break CC.

Rnd 2: [K1 B, p1 MC] around. Break B.

Rnd 3: [K1 D, p1 MC] around. Don't break D.

Rnd 4: [K1 C, p1 MC] around. Break C.

Rnd 5: [K1 D, p1 MC] around. Break D.

Rnd 6: [K1 B, p1 MC] around. Break B.

Rnd 7: [K1 A, p1 MC] around. Don't break A.

Rnd 8: With MC, work in est rib around.

LEG

Rnds 1-2: Knit with MC.

Rnds 3-21: Work Chart. Break D.

Rnds 22-23: Knit with MC.

HEEL FLAP

Row 1 (RS): [K1, sl 1] 11 (12, 13) times, k1, turn—23 (25, 27) heel sts.

Rearrange rem 21 (23, 25) sts on 2 dpns to hold for instep.

Row 2: Purl.

Rep [Rows 1 and 2] 13 (14, 15) times—28 (30, 32) rows with flap measuring approx 2½ (2¾, 3)" [6.5 (7, 7.5)cm]. *Note: For longer heel flap, work more rows, ending with a WS row; when working the gusset, pick up 1 st in each additional slipped st along edge of flap and dec until you reach original st count.*

V-HEEL TURN

Small and large only

Row 1 (RS): [K1, sl 1] 6 (7) times, ssk, k1, turn.

Row 2 (WS): Sl 1, p2, p2tog, p1, turn.

Row 3: [Sl 1, k1] twice, ssk, k1, turn.

Row 4: Sl 1, p4, p2tog, p1, turn.

Row 5: Sl 2, [k1, sl 1] twice, ssk, k1, turn.

Row 6: Sl 1, p6, p2tog, p1, turn.

Row 7: [Sl 1, k1] 4 times, ssk, k1, turn.

Row 8: Sl 1, p8, p2tog, p1, turn.

Row 9: Sl 2, [k1, sl 1] 4 times, ssk, k1, turn.

Row 10: Sl 1, p10, p2tog, p1, turn—13 sts. (end of size small)

Row 11: [Sl 1, k1] 6 times, ssk, k1, turn.

Row 12: Sl 1, p12, p2tog, p1, turn—15 sts. (end of size large)

Medium only

Row 1 (RS): [K1, sl 1] 6 times, k1, ssk, k1, turn.

Row 2 (WS): Sl 1, p2, p2tog, p1, turn.

Row 3: Sl 2, k1, sl 1, ssk, k1, turn.

Row 4: Sl 1, p4, p2tog, p1, turn.

Row 5: [Sl 1, k1] 3 times, ssk, k1, turn.

Row 6: Sl 1, p6, p2tog, p1, turn.

Row 7: Sl 2 [k1, sl 1] 3 times, ssk, k1, turn.

Row 8: Sl 1, p8, p2tog, p1, turn.

Row 9: [Sl 1, k1] 5 times, ssk, k1, turn.

Row 10: Sl 1, p10, p2tog, p1, turn.

Row 11: Sl 2 [k1, sl 1] 5 times, ssk, turn.

Row 12: Sl 1, p11, p2tog, turn—13 sts.

GUSSET

Pick-up rnd: N1: Knit across heel sts, and with the same needle, pick up and knit 14 (15, 16) sts along side of heel flap, then M1 in the "corner" between heel flap and instep; N2: k21 (23, 25) instep sts; N3: M1 in "corner" working it tbl, then pick up and knit 14 (15, 16) sts along other side of heel flap, k6 (6, 7) heel sts from N1; mark beg of rnd—64 (68, 74) sts.

Rnd 1: Knit.

Rnd 2 (dec): N1: Knit to last 3 sts, ssk, k1; N2: knit; N3: k1, k2tog, knit to end of rnd—62 (66, 72) sts.

Rep [Rnds 1 and 2] 9 (9, 10) times—44 (48, 52) sts.

FOOT

Work even in St st until foot measures approx 7¾ (8, 8½)" [19.5 (20.5, 21.5)cm] from back of heel with sock folded flat. *Note: If your feet are shorter/longer, work even until foot measures approx 2½" [5.5cm] short of desired length.*

TOE

Rnd 1: Dec 2 (0, 4) sts evenly around—42 (48, 48) sts.

Rnd 2: *K1, sl 1; rep from * around.

Rnd 3: Knit.

Rnd 4: Rep rnd 2.

Rnd 5: *K5 (6, 6), ssk; rep from * around—36 (42, 42) sts.

Small only

Rnd 6: *[K1, sl 1] 3 times, [sl 1, k1] 3 times; rep from * around.

Rnd 7: Knit.

Rnd 8: Rep Rnd 6.

Medium and large only

Rnd 6: *[K1, sl 1] 3 times, k1; rep from * around.

Rnd 7: Knit.

Rnd 8: Rep rnd 6.

All sizes

Rnd 9: *K4 (5, 5), ssk; rep from * around—30 (36, 36) sts.

Rnd 10: *K1, sl 1; rep from * around.

Rnd 11: Knit.

Rnd 12: Rep rnd 10.

Rnd 13: *K3 (4, 4) sts, ssk; rep from * around—24 (30, 30) sts.

Small only

Rnd 14: *K2, ssk; rep from * around—18 sts.

Rnd 15: *K1, ssk; rep from * around—12 sts.

Rnd 16: Ssk around—6 sts.

Medium and large only

Rnd 14: *[K1, sl 1] twice, k1; rep from * around.

Rnd 15: Knit.

Rnd 16: Rep rnd 14.

Rnd 17: *K3, ssk; rep from * around—24 sts.

Rnd 18: *K2, ssk; rep from * around—18 sts.

Rnd 19: *K1, ssk; rep from * around—12 sts.

Rnd 20: Ssk around—6 sts.

Break yarn, leaving a 6" [15cm] tail. Using tapestry needle, thread tail through rem sts, and pull tight. Weave in all ends.

Block.

COLOR PATTERN

STITCH AND COLOR KEY
- ☐ Knit with MC
- ■ Knit with A
- ▬ Purl with A
- ▨ Knit with B
- ▬ Purl with B
- ☐ Knit with C
- ▨ Knit with D
- ▬ Purl with D

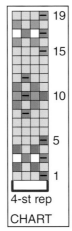

4-st rep

CHART

UPPSALA SOCKS

DESIGN BY CHRISSY GARDINER

Inspired by the wonderful textured colorwork of the Swedish Bohus knitting cooperative, founded by Emma Jacobsson in 1939, these fun, colorful socks integrate purl stitches into the colorwork design for added depth. Traditionally, Bohus designs were knit at nine stitches to the inch on 2.5 mm needles, sometimes including as many as 13 different colors per pattern. ❧

Size
Woman's medium [US Sizes 6–8]

Finished Measurements
Length from cuff to ankle: 4½" [11.5cm]

Foot circumference: 7½" [19cm]

Materials ❶
◆ Alpaca with a Twist *Socrates* (fingering weight; 30% baby alpaca/30% merino wool/20% bamboo/20% nylon; 400 yds [366m] per 3½ oz [100g] ball): 1 ball each Solar Explosion #5016 (MC), Jennifer's Yellow #5017 (A), and Natural #0100 (B)

◆ Size 1 (2.25mm) double-pointed needles (set of 5) or size needed to obtain gauge

◆ Stitch marker

◆ Tapestry needle

Gauge
36 sts and 44 rnds = 4" [10cm] in St st.

Adjust needle size as necessary to obtain correct gauge.

PATTERN NOTES

- This sock is worked from the cuff down with a square heel, gusset, and wedge toe.

- This pattern can be worked using double-pointed needles, two circular needles, or on one long circular needle (using the Magic Loop method). To make the pattern more "universal," needles are not numbered, but stitches are instead referred to as "heel" and "instep." The heel (back of leg/sole) stitches are worked on the first two double-pointed needles or the first circular needle. The instep (front of leg/top of foot) stitches are worked on the last two double-pointed needles or the second circular needle.

- Carry stranded yarn loosely to maintain elasticity of sock.

- Weave in yarn not in use when carrying it more than 3 sts to avoid long floats inside socks.

PATTERN STITCH

See Chart.

INSTRUCTIONS

CUFF

With A, CO 72 sts.

Arrange sts as follows: Place 18 sts on first dpn and 17 sts on second dpn (or 35 sts on first circular needle) for back of leg/heel; place 19 sts on third dpn and 18 sts on forth dpn (or 37 sts on second circular needle) for front of leg/instep. Mark beg of rnd and join, taking care not to twist sts.

Rnds 1–8: *K1 MC, p1 A; rep from * around. Break A.

LEG

Rnds 1–47: Work Rnds 1–17 of chart twice, then work Rnds 1–13 once more. Break B.

HEEL FLAP

Note: The heel flap is worked across the 35 heel sts. If working on dpns, transfer the 35 heel sts to a single dpn (the heel needle). Carry unused yarns on WS throughout heel flap and heel turn.

Row 1 (RS): Sl 1, [k1 MC, p1 A] 16 times, k2 MC.

Row 2: Sl 1, [p1 MC, k1 A] 16 times, p2 MC.

Rep [Rows 1 and 2] 11 more times.

TURN HEEL

Row 1 (RS): Sl 1, [k1 MC, k1 A] 11 times, ssk MC, turn.

Row 2: Sl 1, [p1 A, p1 MC] 5 times, p1 A, p2tog MC, turn.

Row 3: S1 1, [k1 A, k1 MC] 5 times, k1 A, ssk MC, turn.

Row 4: Rep Row 2.

Rep Rows 3 and 4 until all side sts have been worked, ending with a WS row—13 heel sts. Break A.

GUSSET

Pick-up and set-up rnds: Heel/sole sts: with RS facing and working with MC only, knit across 13 heel sts; with same needle, pick up and knit 13 sts along the left edge of heel flap (pick up 1 st in each sl-st chain along edge of heel flap and 1 st in join between heel and instep needles); instep sts: p1, *k1, p1; rep from * across 37 instep sts; heel/sole sts: with empty needle, pick up and knit 13 sts down right edge of heel flap as before, then k7 sts from second needle so that heel/sole sts are divided evenly over the two heel needles; knit to end of heel sts; work 37 instep sts in est rib—76 sts with beg of rnd between 37 instep and 39 heel/sole sts.

Rnd 1: Heel/sole: knit to last 3 sts, k2tog, k1; instep: work in est rib—75 sts.

Rnd 2: Heel/sole: k1, ssk, knit to end of heel sts; instep: work in est rib—74 sts.

Rep [Rnds 1 and 2] once more—72 sts.

FOOT

Work sole sts in St st and instep sts in est rib until foot measures 3" [7.5cm] short of desired length.

Next 12 rnds: Work Rnds 1–12 of chart. Break B.

Next rnd: With MC, knit across sole sts; k1, ssk, knit to last 3 instep sts, k2tog, k1—70 sts.

TOE

Rnd 1: *[K1 MC, k1 A] to last sole st, k1 MC; rep from * across instep sts.

Rnd 2 (dec): *K1 MC, ssk A, [k1 A, k1 MC] to last 4 sole sts, k1 A, k2tog A, k1 MC; rep from * across instep sts—66 sts.

Rnd 3: *K1 MC, k2 A, [k1 MC, k1 A] to last 2 sole sts, k1 A, k1 MC; rep from * across instep sts.

Rnd 4 (dec): *K1 MC, ssk A, [k1 MC, k1 A] to last 4 sole sts, k1 MC, k2tog A, k1; rep from * across instep sts—62 sts.

Cont working in this manner, maintaining stripe pat with 1 st MC at each end of instep and sole and working decs with A; work decs every other rnd until 38 sts rem, then work decs every rnd until 22 sts rem (11 sts each instep and sole).

FINISHING

Break yarns, leaving MC tail of 14–18" [35–45cm].

With tapestry needle and MC tail, graft toe closed using Kitchener st.

Weave in all ends. Block.

COLOR PATTERN

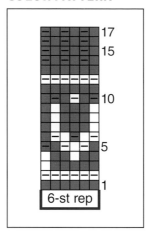

6-st rep

STITCH AND COLOR KEY
- Knit with MC
- Purl with MC
- Knit with B
- Purl with B

FINNISH PÄIVÄTÄR SOCKS

DESIGN BY HEATHER ANNE ORDOVER

Päivätär is the name of the Sun Goddess in the Finnish epic poem, *The Kalevala*. Not only was Päivätär the sun goddess, but she was also the goddess of spinning, and and her sister, the goddess of the moon, was in charge of weaving. In this pattern you'll see sun discs slide down the side seams and turn into little twists—like plies—leading down to the toes. The trellis pattern in the cuff was used in both knitting and weaving.

Traditional Finnish textiles have historically focused more on weaving than knitting, which can be seen in the geometric nature of many Finnish designs. The cuff, the purled side-seam textures, and the traveling stitches seen on this sock are, indeed, patterns and techniques that were historically used in Finland.

In recent times, traditional Finnish costumes have included the bright red skirts and vests, headbands, white stockings, and black shoes of the late ninteteenth century.

Size
Woman's medium [US size 6–8] /man's small [US size 5–9]. Instructions are given for one size, with suggestions for making smaller/larger sizes in Pattern Notes.

Finished Measurements
Length from cuff to ankle: 9"/23cm

Foot circumference: 8.5"/21.5cm

Materials ❶
◆ The March Hare *Wool* (fingering weight; 100%wool; 440 yds [402m] per 3½oz [100g] ball): One ball Cream (A)

◆ The March Hare *Silk Blend* (fingering weight; 70% merino/30% silk; 435 yds [398m] per 3 oz [100g] ball): 1 ball each Scarlet Letter (B) and Balsam (C)

◆ Size 0 [2mm] circular needles (2) or size needed to obtain gauge

◆ Stitch markers

◆ Tapestry needle

Gauge
28 sts and 44 rnds = 4" [10cm] in St st.

Adjust needle size as necessary to obtain correct gauge.

PATTERN NOTES

♦ This sock is worked from the cuff down, with leg shaping, an outside "seam" panel, a Dutch (square) heel, and a wedge toe. The top cuff edge has a "plaited" pattern.

♦ The pattern is written assuming that the sock is worked on two circular needles. It could just as easily be worked using the Magic Loop method or on four double-pointed needles.

♦ The Cuff-Seam Pattern is bordered by vertical bands of B. When working the twisted purl stitches of the Side-Seam Pattern, those border stitches can either be worked as regular knit stitches or as twisted knit stitches (k1-tbl) to give a firm edge to the Side-Seam pattern.

♦ Strand the yarn not in use loosely on wrong side to maintain elasticity of fabric; do not carry yarn not in use more than 5 sts—weave it in as necessary.

♦ Adjusting for size: the cuff as written will fit a 10–11½" [25.5–29cm] calf. If smaller/larger cuff size is desired, decrease/increase in the Cuff-Seam Pattern. Eliminating the Cuff-Seam pattern would create a woman's small. To create a larger woman's sock, insert an additional Cuff-Seam Pattern between two repeats of the 18-st cuff pattern. Adjust heel flap accordingly.

SPECIAL ABBREVIATIONS

RT (Right Twist): Knit into front of the second st on LH needle, then into first st; slip both sts off.

N1 and N2: Needle 1 and Needle 2 with N1 holding heel/sole sts and N2 holding instep sts.

Double-Purl Stitch (optional): This can be substituted for any twisted purl stitch (p1-tbl) in the pattern. It gives a slightly more pronounced purl bump and extra reinforcement. Work as follows: Bring yarn to the front; sl 1 pwise; bring yarn to back; pass slipped st back to LH needle; p1.

Prior to that, knitted stockings would have been the norm, but were sometimes more like leg warmers and were used for propriety, because actual foot coverings were often considered unnecessary in the summertime. ❧

STITCH PATTERNS

CUFF PATTERN (18-ST REP)

See Chart, page 35

CUFF-SEAM PATTERN (9-ST PANEL)

See Chart, page 35

SIDE-SEAM PATTERN (9-ST PANEL)

Note: Double-purl st can be substituted for purling tbl.

Rnd 1: K1-tbl, k3, p1-tbl, k3, k1-tbl.

Rnd 2: K1-tbl, k2, p3-tbl, k2, k1-tbl.

Rnd 3: K1-tbl, k1, p2-tbl, k1, p2-tbl, k1, k1-tbl.

Rnd 4: K1-tbl, p2-tbl, k3, p2-tbl, k1-tbl.

Rnd 5: K1-tbl, p1-tbl, k5, p1-tbl, k1-tbl.

Rnd 6: K1-tbl, p2-tbl, k3, p2-tbl, k1-tbl.

Rnd 7: K1-tbl, k1, p2-tbl, k1, p2-tbl, k1, k1-tbl.

Rnd 8: K1-tbl, k2, p3-tbl, k2, k1-tbl.

Rep Rnds 1–8 at for pat.

CLOCK

See Chart, page 35

Note: For longer leg, rep Rnd 15 until you reach desired length.

MINI-CABLE (4-ST PANEL)

Rnds 1–3: P1, k2, p1.

Rnd 4: P1, RT, p1.

Rep Rnds 1–4 for pat.

LEFT SOCK

Cuff

Holding A and B tog, make a slipknot on needle. Using long-tail method and holding B over your index finger and A over your thumb, CO 82 sts; remove slipknot from needle. Distribute sts so that there are 40 sts on first circular needle and 42 sts on second circular needle. Mark beg of rnd.

Plaited Edge

Rnd 1: With yarns in back, *k1 A, k1 B; rep from * around.

Rnd 2: With yarns in front and bringing working yarn over the previous color, *p1 A, p1 B; rep from * around. *Note: Yarns will twist on this rnd, but will untwist on Rnd 3.*

Rnd 3: With yarns in front and bringing working yarn *under* previous color, *p1 A, p1 B; rep from * around.

Rnd 4: With yarns in back, *k1 A, p1 B; rep from * around. Break B.

Ribbing

With A, work K1, P1 Rib for 11 rnds and on last rnd, pull last st of rnd over first st of rnd—81 sts with 40 sts on N1 and 41 sts on N2.

Color Patterns

Rnd 1 (set-up): Work 4 reps of 18-st Cuff pat to last 9 sts, pm; work 9-st Cuff-Seam pat.

Rnds 2-29: Work even in est pats (end of Cuff-Seam pat).

Rnd 30: Work est Cuff pat, sm, with A, k9.

Rnds 31-32: Work est Cuff pat, sm, work 9-st Side-Seam pat.

Leg

Rnd 33: Work P1, K1 Rib to 2 sts before marker, p2tog; sm, work Side-Seam pat—80 sts with 40 sts on each needle.

Rnds 34-43: Work 10 rnds in est pats.

Dec rnd: K1, ssk, knit to 3 sts before marker, k2tog, k1, sm, work Side-Seam pat—78 sts.

Cont in St st and Side-Seam pat and rep Dec rnd [every 3rd rnd] 7 more times—64 sts with 32 sts on each needle.

Work even until 6 reps of 8-rnd Side-Seam pat are complete.

Next 15 rnds: Knit to marker, sm, work 9-st Clock pat.

Next rnd: N1: Knit to last 3 sts, then slip those sts to N2; N2: knit the 3 slipped sts from N1, work in est pat (including Rnd 16 of Clock pat) to last 3 sts; slip last 3 sts to N1 for new beg of rnd.

Next rnd: N1: Complete Clock pat on first 3 sts, knit to end; N2: knit to marker, p1, RT, p2tog, k1—31 sts on N2.

Heel Flap

Worked on N1 only; sts on N2 rem on hold for instep.

Row 1 (RS): Ssk with A, *k1 A, k1 B; rep from * to last 2 sts, k2 A—31 sts.

Row 2 (WS): Sl 1, *p1 A, p1 B; rep from * to last 2 sts, p2 A.

Row 3: Sl 1, *k1 A, k1 B; rep from * to last 2 sts, k2 A.

Rep [Rows 2 and 3] 14 times, then work Row 2 once more—32 rows total.

Turn Heel

Work in est color pat, making all decs with B.

Row 1 (RS): Sl 1, k21 in est pat, ssk with B, turn, leaving 7 sts unworked.

Row 2 (WS): Sl 1, p13, p2tog with B, turn, leaving 7 sts unworked.

Row 3: Sl 1, k13, ssk with B, turn.

Row 4: Rep Row 2.

Rep Rows 3 and 4 until all sts have been worked, ending with a WS row—15 sts.

Break yarns.

Gusset

Set-up rnd: N1: With RS facing and A, beg at outer corner (clock side) between instep and flap, pick up and knit 16 sts along heel flap; knit across 15 heel sts; pick up and knit 16 sts along other side of flap; N2: knit to last 5 sts, pm, work Mini-Cable pat, k1; mark beg of rnd—78 sts with 47 sts on N1 and 31 sts on N2.

Dec rnd: N1: Ssk, knit to last 2 sts, k2tog; N2: work in est pats—76 sts.

Cont in est pats and rep Dec rnd [every other rnd] 8 times—60 sts with 29 sts on N1 and 31 sts on N2.

Foot

Work even in est pats until foot measures approx 6½" [16.5cm] from back of heel or 2" [5cm] short of desired length.

Next rnd: N1: Knit across; N2: k1, ssk, knit to last 3 sts, k2tog, k1—58 sts with 29 sts on each needle.

Toe

Rnd 1: N1: K2 B, *k1 A, k1 B; rep from * last st, k1 B; N2: work as for N1.

Rnd 2 (dec): N1: K1 B, ssk with B, work est color pat to last 3 sts, k2tog with B, k1 B; N2: work as for N1—54 sts.

Rep [Rnds 1 and 2] 8 more times—22 sts.

Break yarns, leaving a 6" [15cm] tail for A and a 12" [30.5cm] tail for B.

With tapestry needle and B, graft toe closed using Kitchener st.

RIGHT SOCK

Work as for Left Sock until 15 rnds of Clock chart are complete.

Next rnd: N1: Knit to last 6 sts, then slip those sts to N2. This is new beg of rnd; N2 now becomes N1 and N1 becomes N2.

Next rnd: N1: Knit the 6 slipped sts, work in est pat (including Rnd 16 of Clock pat) to last 6 sts; slip last 6 sts to N2; N2: complete Clock pat, knit to end.

Heel Flap

Worked on N1 only; sts on N2 rem on hold for instep.

Row 1 (RS): Sl 1, *k1 A, k1 B; rep from * to last 3 sts, k2tog A, k1 A—31 sts.

Continue as for Left Sock.

Heel Turn

Work as for Left Sock.

Gusset

Set-up rnd: N1: With RS facing and A, beg at inner corner (non-clock side) between instep and flap, pick up and knit 16 sts along heel flap; knit across 15 heel sts; pick up and knit 16 sts along other side of flap; N2: k1, p2tog, RT, p1, knit to end; mark beg of rnd—78 sts with 47 sts on N1 and 31 sts on N2.

Dec rnd: N1: Ssk, knit to last 2 sts, k2tog; N2: k1, work Mini-Cable pat, knit to end—76 sts.

Cont in est pats and rep Dec rnd [every other rnd] 8 times—60 sts with 29 sts on N1 and 31 sts on N2.

Leg and Toe

Work as for Left Sock.

FINISHING

Weave in all ends. Block. Steam side seams lightly if needed.

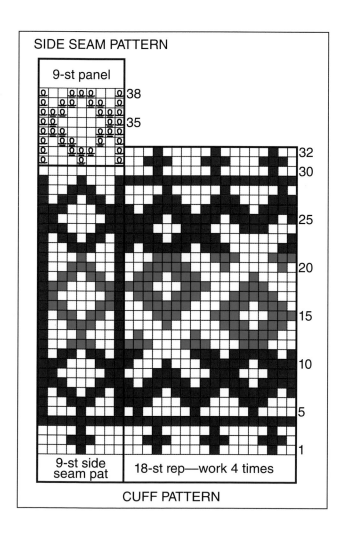

SIDE SEAM PATTERN

9-st panel

9-st side seam pat

18-st rep—work 4 times

CUFF PATTERN

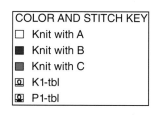

COLOR AND STITCH KEY
- ☐ Knit with A
- ■ Knit with B
- ▨ Knit with C
- Ⓠ K1-tbl
- Ⓠ P1-tbl

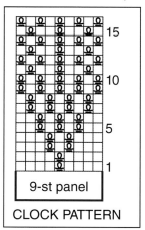

9-st panel

CLOCK PATTERN

NORWEGIAN SOCKS

DESIGN BY KRISTIN SPURKLAND

Inspired by memories of childhood hikes in the forests and on the fjords in Norway (and the hand-knit socks my relatives wore on those hikes), these socks utilize traditional Norwegian patterns and colors. The design features a Selbu Star, a popular motif in the Norwegian knitting tradition. Although the patterning is complex, the gusset panels on the calves and the herringbone pattern down the back of the leg allow for achieving a customized fit without much trouble. ❧

Size
Woman's medium [US size 8–9]

Finished Measurements
Foot circumference: 8" [20.5cm]

Calf circumference: 14½" [37cm]

Foot length: 9" [23cm]

Materials 🧶**1**
◆ ShibuiKnits *Sock* (fingering weight; 65% superwash merino/30% silk/5% nylon; 191 yds [175m] per 1¾ oz [50g] skein): 3 skeins Midnight (A), two skeins Ivory (B)

◆ Size 1 [2.25mm] double-pointed needles (set of 5)

◆ Size 3 [3.25mm] double-pointed needles (set of 5) or size needed to obtain gauge

◆ Stitch markers

◆ Tapestry needle

Gauge
32 sts and 32 rnds = 4" [10cm] in stranded St st.

Adjust needle size as necessary to obtain correct gauge.

PATTERN NOTES

- This sock is worked from the cuff down, with a shaped calf gusset, a flap heel, and a wedge toe.
- Variations in fit can be achieved by adjusting needle size up or down. For thinner calves, ribbing may be worked on smaller needle; for thicker calves, work ribbing on larger needle.
- The calf can also be adjusted by adding or subtracting sts in the calf-gusset panels.
- For smaller socks, the main pattern can be knit on smaller needles.
- For the best results, try on the sock several times while knitting, to ensure the desired fit is being achieved, and adjust needle size/stitch count as necessary.
- Strand the yarn not in use loosely on WS to maintain elasticity of fabric; do not carry yarn not in use more than 5 sts—weave it in as necessary.

INSTRUCTIONS

CUFF

With smaller needles and A, CO 84 sts. Distribute sts evenly on 4 dpns; mark beg of rnd and join, taking care not to twist sts.

Work in K2, P2 Rib for 4" [10cm].

Next rnd: Change to larger dpns; knit and inc 20 sts evenly around—104 sts.

LEG

Set-up rnd: Work Calf Chart over first 39 sts; k7 A for gusset panel and mark center st; k1 B, work Main Pattern Chart over next 49 sts, k1 B; k7 A for gusset panel and mark center st.

Rnds 2-6: Work pats and colors as est.

SHAPE CALF

Gusset Inc Rnd: *Work est pats to marked center st of gusset panel, M1, k1, M1; rep from * once, work to end—108 sts.

Maintaining est pats, rep Gusset Inc Rnd [every 5th rnd] twice, working new sts with A—116 sts.

Work even until Rnd 6 of 2nd rep of Main pat is complete.

Gusset Dec Rnd: *Work to 1 st before marked center st of gusset panel, S2K2P; rep from * once, work to end—112 sts.

Maintaining est pat, rep Gusset Dec Rnd [every 3rd rnd] 6 times, and on the last Gusset Dec Rnd, work the dec with B—88 sts with all gusset sts eliminated and 1 st B each side between Calf pat and Main pat.

Work even until Rnd 3 of third rep of Main pat is complete.

Calf Dec Rnd: Work to 1 st before center st of Calf Panel, S2KP2 with B, work to end of rnd—86 sts.

Maintaining est pat, rep Calf Dec Rnd [every 3rd rnd] 11 times—64 sts.

Work even until 4 reps of Main pat are complete. Break both yarns.

HEEL FLAP

Set up: Slip first 23 sts of rnd onto 1 dpn for heel; place next 33 sts onto 2 dpns for instep; slip last 8 sts to heel dpn—31 heel sts on 1 dpn.

Row 1 (WS): With the WS facing, join A and purl a row.

Row 2 (RS): *Sl 1, k1; rep from * to last st, k1.

Row 3: Sl 1, purl to end.

Rep [Rows 2 and 3] 15 times.

TURN HEEL

Row 1 (RS): K18, k2tog, k1, turn.

Row 2: Sl 1, p6, p2tog, p1.

Row 3: Sl 1, k7, ssk, k1.

Row 4: Sl 1, p8, p2tog, p1.

Row 5: Sl 1, 98, ssk, k1.

Row 6: Sl 1, p10, p2tog, p1.

Cont in this manner until all the heel sts have been worked—19 heel sts rem.

Break yarn.

HEEL GUSSET

Pick-up rnd: With spare dpn (N1) and A, and beg at point where right-hand side of flap (as you are looking at it) meets instep sts, pick up and knit 10 st along flap, then with A and B, pick up 6 sts following Sole Chart; knit 8 heel sts continuing Sole Chart; with another dpn (N2), knit rem 9 heel sts following Sole Chart, then pick up and knit 6 sts along left side of flap, ending Sole Chart; with A, pick up 10 sts to end of flap; N3 and N4: work 33 instep sts following Instep Chart—84 sts with 10 gusset sts each side and 31 sole sts on N1 and N2 and 33 instep sts on N3 and N4.

Rnd 1: N1: Ssk, work in est pats to end; N2: work in est pats to last 2 sts, k2tog; N3 and N4: work est Instep pat—82 sts.

Rnd 2: Work even in est pats.

Rep [Rnds 1 and 2] 8 times—66 sts.

Next rnd: N1: K2tog with B, work to end; N2: work to last 2 sts, ssk with B; N3 and N4: work est Instep pat—64 sts with 31 sole sts and 33 instep sts.

FOOT

Work even in est pats until Instep Chart has been worked twice, or until foot is approximately 2½" [6.5cm] short of desired length.

Break B.

TOE

Rnd 1: Knit with A only.

Rnd 2: N1 and N2: knit; N3: k1, ssk, knit to end; N4: knit to last 3 sts, k2tog, k1—62 sts.

Rnd 3: *N1: k1, ssk, knit to end; N2: knit to last 3 sts, k2tog, k1; N3 and N4: rep from *—58 sts.

Rep [Rnd 3] 9 times—22 sts.

FINISHING

Break yarn, leaving a 12" [30.5cm] tail. Transfer sts on N2 to N1 and sts on N4 to N3—11 sts on each needle. With tapestry needle and tail, graft toe closed using Kitchener st. Weave in ends. Block sock.

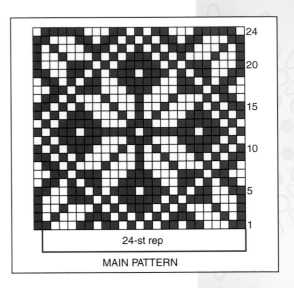

24
20
15
10
5
1

24-st rep

MAIN PATTERN

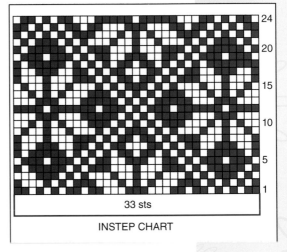

24
20
15
10
5
1

33 sts

INSTEP CHART

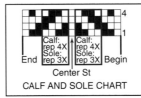

4
1

Calf: rep 4X Sole: rep 3X   Calf: rep 4X Sole: rep 3X

End   Begin

Center St

CALF AND SOLE CHART

COLOR KEY
■ A
□ B

ICELANDIC SOCKS

DESIGN BY HÉLÈNE MAGNÚSSON

Traditional Icelandic socks were usually knitted to shape from the top down. The heel flap was very common, as well as a wedge toe. The cuff was often ribbed and the calf shaped with increases and decreases on both sides of a purl row at the back of the leg. A few short rows were sometimes added at the instep to make it slightly longer than the sole and thus more comfortable. With the exception of the wedge toe, I retained all those details in my design.

Icelandic socks were largely very plain, barely decorated with a few stripes. It seems that all the embellishment was on the bands that were braided around the legs to hold the socks in place, so this is where I concentrated my efforts. The sockbands were woven—mostly with tablet weaving—in many colors, with all sorts of motifs, and often the initials or the name of its owner. I interpreted these bands as a knitted color band with typical motifs and initials. The old

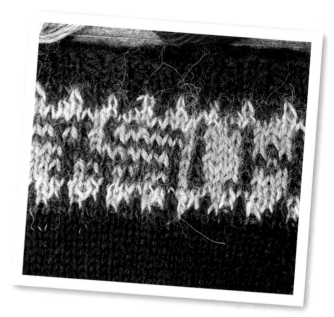

Sizes

Woman's medium [US sizes 6–8] (woman's large [US sizes 8–12]/man's medium [US sizes 10½–12]). Instructions are given for smaller size, with larger size in parentheses. When only 1 number is given, it applies to both sizes.

Finished Measurements

Foot circumference: 8¼ (9)" [21(23)cm]

Calf circumference (widest): 13¼ (14)" [34 (36)cm]

Foot length: 9 (10½)" [23 (26)cm]

Length from cuff to heel: 16 (17)" [40.5 (45.5)cm]

Materials ⓵

◆ Lana Grossa *Meilenweit Merino* (fingering weight; 80% merino wool/20% polyamide; 462 yds [420m] per 3½ oz [100g] ball): 1 ball Navy Blue #2011 (MC), approx 10 yds Tan #1290 (A)

◆ Ístex *Loðband-Einband* (lace weight; 100% new wool; 245 yds [225m] per 1¾ oz [50g] ball): approx 10 yds [9m] each Light Beige Heather #1038 (B), Crimson #0047 (C), and Black Sheep (D)

◆ Size 1 [2.25mm] double-pointed needles (set of 5)

◆ Size 2 [2.75mm] double-pointed needles (set of 5) or size needed to obtain gauge

◆ Stitch markers

◆ Tapestry needle

GAUGE

26 sts and 36 rows = 4" [10cm] in St st on larger needles with MC.

Adjust needle size as necessary to obtain correct gauge. You can obtain more sizes by playing with the needle sizes, using smaller or larger needles.

PATTERN NOTES

- These socks are worked from the cuff down, with a shaped calf, back leg "seam," heel flap, round heel, gusset, a short-rowed instep, and spiral toe.

- Because the socks are worked from the cuff down, the motifs are worked upside down. Knit your initials upside down in the empty space of the chart—the alphabet chart is presented upside down for your convenience.

- Since leg/calf measurements vary widely, you may choose to adapt the pattern to your leg either by using different needles or by altering the stitch count of the patterned band by playing with the center front motif. If you revise the stitch count, remember to change the rate and number of increase/decrease rounds accordingly.

- When working the patterned band, use your favorite method to avoid the color job between rounds.

- Strand the yarn not in use loosely on wrong side to maintain elasticity of fabric; do not carry yarn not in use more than 4 sts—weave it in as necessary.

SPECIAL ABBREVIATIONS

N1, N2, N3, N4: Needle 1, needle 2, needle 3, needle 4, with N1 and N4 holding sole sts and N2 and N3 holding instep sts.

Icelandic alphabet chart will allow you how to customize your socks with your own initials or with the initials of the person for whom the socks are intended. ❧

STITCH PATTERNS

BACK LEG PATTERN—WOMAN'S (7 STS)

Rnd 1: K1, ssk, yo, p1, yo, k2tog, k1.

Rnd 2: Knit.

Rep Rows 1 and 2 for pat.

BACK LEG PATTERN—MAN'S (7 STS)

Pattern rnd: K3, p1, k3.

INSTRUCTIONS

CUFF

With MC and smaller needle, CO 72 (78) sts. Distribute sts evenly among 4 dpns; mark beg of rnd and join, taking care not to twist sts.

Work K2, P2 Rib for 3 rnds.

Knit 1 rnd.

Work Patterned Band Chart, working your initials upside down on the empty space on the chart.

LEG

Change to larger dpns and MC.

Shape calf

Set-up rnd: With MC, k8, place marker, work Back Leg pat over next 7 sts, place marker, knit to end of rnd.

Inc rnd: Knit to marker, M1, work Back Leg pat to marker, M1, knit to end—74 (80) sts.
Maintaining Back Leg pat between markers, rep Inc rnd [every other rnd] 7 times—88 (94) sts.

Work even for 8 (9) rnds.

Dec rnd: Knit to 2 sts before marker, ssk, work Back Leg pat, k2tog, knit to end—86 (92) sts.
Maintaining pat between markers, rep Dec rnd [every 5 rnds] 16 times—54 (60) sts.

Work 14 (23) rnds even or until leg is desired length to heel, ending last rnd 2 (3 sts) before end of rnd.

HEEL FLAP

Row 1 (RS): Removing markers, sl 1, k26 (29) for heel; leave rem 27 (30) sts on hold for instep.

Row 2: Sl 1, purl to end.

Row 3: Sl 1, knit to end.

Rep [Rows 2 and 3] 9 (10) times.

TURN HEEL

Row 1 (WS): Sl 1, p15 (16), p2tog, p1; turn.

Row 2: Sl 1, k6 (5), ssk, k1; turn.

Row 3: Sl 1, purl to 1 st before gap, p2tog (1 st from each side of the gap), p1; turn.

Row 4: Sl 1, knit to 1 st before gap, ssk (1 st from each side of the gap), k1; turn.

Rep Rows 3 and 4 until all sts have been worked and 17 (18) sts remain.

GUSSET

Rnd 1: N1: With needle holding heel sts, pick up and knit 10 (11) sl sts along edge of heel flap, M1 in corner between flap and instep; N2: k14 (15) instep sts; N3: k13 (15) instep sts; N4: M1 in corner between flap and instep, pick up and knit 10 (11) sl sts along edge of heel flap, knit 8 (9) sts from N1 (new beg of rnd)—66 (72) sts.

Rnd 2: N1: Knit to last 3 sts, k2tog, k1; N2 and N3: knit across; N4: k1, ssk, knit to end—64 (70) sts.

Rnd 3: Knit around.

Rep [Rnds 2 and 3] 10 times—54 (60) sts.

FOOT

Work 10 (15) rnds even.

Instep-short-row rnd: Knit to end of N3, turn; yo, purl to end of N2, turn; yo, knit to first yo, k2tog [yo and next st], knit to end of rnd.

Next rnd: Knit to 1 st before yo, ssk [st and yo], knit to end of rnd.

Knit 9 (14) rnds, then rep Instep-short-row rnd.

Work even until foot measures 7¼ (8¼)" [18 (21)cm] or 2" [5cm] short of desired length.

SPIRAL TOE

Rnd 1: *K2tog, yo, k7 (8); rep from * around.

Rnd 2 and all even rnds: Knit around.

Rnd 3 (size L only): *K2tog, yo, k2tog, k6; rep from * around—54 sts.

Rnd 3 (5): *K2tog, yo, k2tog, k5; rep from * around—48 sts.

Rnd 5 (7): *K2tog, yo, k2tog, k4; rep from * around—42 sts.

Rnd 7 (9): *K2tog, yo, k2tog, k3*; rep from * around—36 sts.

Rnd 9 (11): *K2tog, yo, k2tog, k2; rep from * around—30 sts.

Rnd 11 (13): *K2tog, yo, k2tog, k1; rep from * around—24 sts.

Rnd 13 (15): *K2tog, yo, k2tog; rep from * around—18 sts.

Rnd 15 (17): *K1, k2tog; rep from * around—12 sts.

Rnd 17 (19): *K1, k2tog; rep form * around—8 sts.

FINISHING

Break yarn, leaving a 6" [15cm] tail. Using tapestry needle, thread tail through rem sts and pull tight. Weave in all ends. Block.

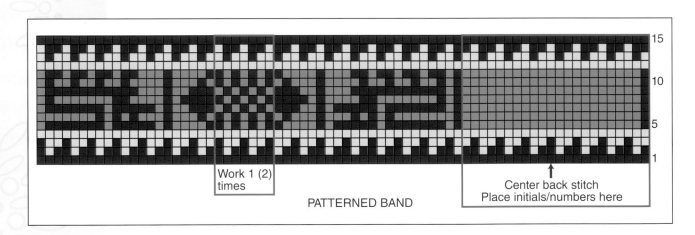

Work 1 (2) times

PATTERNED BAND

Center back stitch
Place initials/numbers here

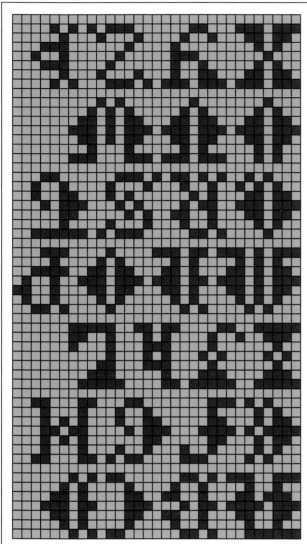

ALPHABET CHART FOR INITIALS

Note: Initials are worked upside down

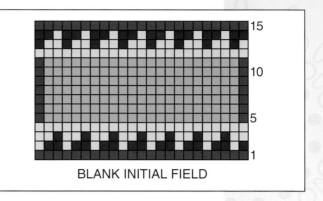

BLANK INITIAL FIELD

15

10

5

1

COLOR KEY
A
B
C
D

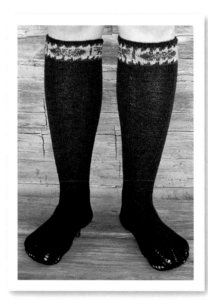

SOCKS OF
THE BRITISH ISLES

Jane Jones in Welsh Costume.

GANSEY SOCKS

DESIGN BY BETH BROWN-REINSEL

These Gansey Socks were inspired by the wonderful fisherman sweaters created in Britain in the nineteenth century. The construction includes a back seam made of a baby cable, starfish, and panels with diagonal lines; a slip-stitch heel; a square (German) heel turning; wedge-toe shaping; and Kitchener stitch for finishing the toes. The socks feature the classic Channel Island Cast-On. This decorative and substantial cast-on forms a strand of "beads" along the beginning edge of the garment that accentuates, by contrast, the horizontal lines of a garter welt. 🖒

Size
Woman's medium [US shoe size 8–9]

Finished Measurements
Length from cuff to ankle: 6½" [16.5cm]

Length from cuff to heel: 9⅜" [24 cm]

Foot circumference: 8" [20.5cm]

Materials 🔒2
◆ Frangipani *5-ply Guernsey Wool* (sport weight; 100% wool; 1200 yds [1097m] per 17¾ oz [500g] cone): approx 300 yds [274m]. Shown in Amethyst. You can substitute any sport-weight wool yarn for a firm, warm sock, or a fingering-weight sock yarn for a lighter sock.

◆ Size 2 (2.75mm) double-pointed needles (set of 4) or size needed to obtain gauge

◆ Tapestry needle

Gauge
28 sts and 40 rnds = 4" [10cm] in St st.

Adjust needle size as necessary to obtain correct gauge.

PATTERN NOTES

- This sock is worked with 4 double-point needles from the cuff down with a heel flap, German/square heel turn, and a wedge toe.

- The needles are identified as N1, N2, and N3 in the order that they are used. After the leg is worked, the heel flap stitches (centered above the back mini-cable seam) are put on N3, with the instep stitches remaining on hold on N1 and N2. When working the foot, N1 and N3 hold the heel/gusset/sole sts and N2 holds the instep sts.

SPECIAL TECHNIQUE

THE CHANNEL ISLAND CAST-ON

The slipknot itself is made of three loops formed from three strands of yarn held as one. When working this method, do not count the slipknot—you can remove and pull out that first stitch after the first round has been worked without harm to the rest of your stitches.

This technique forms two stitches at once. Two strands of yarn are used together to wind around the thumb forming the bead, while a third strand is used to form the stitches. You can use both ends of one skein plus one end from a piece broken off from your ball (about 60" [152cm] long).

SPECIAL ABBREVIATIONS

Tw2R (Twist 2 Right): K2tog but do not remove from LH needle. Knit into the first st again and take both st s off left needle.

N1, N2, N3: Needle 1, needle 2, needle 3

STITCH PATTERN

A chart is provided for those who prefer working from charts.

Rnd 1: P1, k2, p1, k2, [p1, k1] 3 times, k7, [p1, k1] 3 times, k16, [p1, k1] 3 times, k7, [p1, k1] 3 times, k1.

Rnd 2: P1, k2, p1, k8, p1, k39, p1, k8.

Rnd 3: P1, Tw2R, p1, k2, [p1, k1] 3 times, p2, k5, [p1, k1] 3 times, k4, p1, k5, p1, k5, [p1, k1] 3 times, k4, p2, k1, [p1, k1] 3 times, k1.

Rnd 4: P1, k2, p1, k9, p2, k14, p2, k3, p2, k14, p2, k9.

Rnd 5: P1, k2, p1, k2, [p1, k1] 3 times, k2, p2, k3, [p1, k1] 3 times, k4, p3, k1, p3, k5, [p1, k1] 3 times, k2, p2, k3, [p1, k1] 3 times, k1.

Rnd 6: P1, k2, p1, k11, p2, k13, p2, k1, p2, k13, p2, k11.

Rnd 7: P1, Tw2R, p1, k2, [p1, k1] 3 times, k4, p2, k1 [p1, k1] 3 times, k6, p1, k1, p1, k7, [p1, k1] 3 times, p2, k5, [p1, k1] 3 times, k1.

Rnd 8: P1, k2, p1, k13, p1, k8, p3, k7, p3, k8, p1, k13.

Rnd 9: P1, k2, p1, k2, [p1, k1] 3 times, k7, [p1, k1] 3 times, k2, p3, k5, p3, k3, [p1, k1] 3 times, k7, [p1, k1] 3 times, k1.

Rnd 10: P1, k2, p1, k24, p3, k3, p3, k24.

Rnd 11: P1, Tw2R, p1, k2, [p1, k1] 3 times, k7, [p1, k1] 3 times, k4, p3, k1, p3, k5 [p1, k1] 3 times, k7, [p1. k1] 3 times, k1.

Rnd 12: P1, k2, p1, k8, p1, k15, p3, k3, p3, k15, p1, k8.

Rnd 13: P1, k2, p1, k2, [p1, k1] 3 times, p2, k5, [p1, k1] 3 times, k2, p3, k5, p3, k3, [p1, k1] 3 times, k4, p2, k1, [p1, k1] 3 times, k1.

Rnd 14: P1, k2, p1, k9, p2, k11, p3, k7, p3, k11, p2, p9.

Rnd 15: P1, Tw2R, p1, k2, [p1, k1] 3 times, k2, p2, k3, [p1, k1] 3 times, k6, p1, k1, p1, k7, [p1, k1] 3 times, k2, p2, k3, [p1, k1] 3 times, k1.

Rnd 16: P1, k2, p1, k11, p2, k13, p2, k1, p2, k13, p2, k11.

Rnd 17: P1, k2, p1, k2, [p1, k1] 3 times, k4, p2, k1, [p1, k1] 3 times, k4, p3, k1, p3, k5, [p1, k1] 3 times, p2, k5, [p1, k1] 3 times, k1.

Rnd 18: P1, k2, p1, k13, p1, k11, p2, k3, p2, k11, p1, k13.

Rnd 19: P1, Tw2R, p1, k2, [p1, k1] 3 times, k7, [p1, k1] 3times, k4, p1, k5, p1, k5, [p1, k1] 3 times, k7, [p1, k1] 3 times, k1.

Rnd 20: P1, k2, p1, knit to end of rnd.

Rep Rnds 1-20 for pat.

INSTRUCTIONS

Using the Channel Island method, cast on 54 sts, dividing sts evenly among 3 dpns: 18-18-18. Remove slipknot and join, being careful not to twist.

GARTER WELT

Rnd 1: Knit, increasing 7 sts evenly around—61 sts divided 20-21-20.

Rnds 2 and 4: Purl.

Rnd 3: Knit.

LEG

Work 20-rnd pat 3 times—60 rnds.

RE-ARRANGE STS FOR HEEL FLAP AND INSTEP STS

With N3, work 18 sts from N1 (2 sts left on N1); sl 13 sts from N2 to N1; sl 6 sts from N3 to N2—sts now arranged 15-14-32. The 32 sts on N3 are heel sts; the rem 29 sts will be held for the instep.

HEEL FLAP

Turn your work so that the WS of the heel is facing you; work heel sts back and forth in rows.

Row 1 (WS): Sl 1 pwise wyif, purl to end.

Row 2 (RS): *Sl 1 pwise wyib, k1, rep from * to end.

Rep [Rows 1 and 2] 13 times—28 rows.

Purl 1 row.

HEEL TURN

Row 1 (RS): K20, ssk, turn.

Row 2: Sl 1 pwise, p8, p2tog, turn.

Row 3: Sl 1 pwise, k8, ssk, turn.

Rep Rows 2 and 3 until 10 sts rem ready to work a RS row.

GUSSET

Slip 29 instep sts to 1 dpn (now N2).

Rnd 1: N1: K10 heel sts, then pick up and knit 17 sts along the side of the heel flap; N2: beg with Row 1, work charted pat across 29 instep sts; N3: pick up and knit 17 sts down other side of heel flap, then k5 from N1—73 sts distributed as 22-29-22. The beg of rnd is now at center heel/sole.

Rnd 2: N1: K21, then slip last st to N2; N2: k2tog, work in est pat across 27 sts, work an ssk with the last st of N2 and the first st of N3; N3: k21—71 sts. Note: This rnd eliminates the gap between the instep and heel sts.

Rnd 3: N1: Knit to last 3 sts, k2tog, k1; N2: work 29 sts of pat on instep; N3: k1, ssk, k18—69 sts.

Rnd 4: Work even in est pats (Gansey pat on instep sts, St st on sole sts).

Rep [Rnds 3 and 4] 4 times—61 sts distributed as 16-29-16.

FOOT

Work even in est pats until 3 reps of instep pat are complete. *Note: Three reps yields a sock which will fit a woman wearing a US size 8–9 shoe. To adjust for length, knit all rounds after the 3rd rep until foot measures 2½" [6.5cm] shorter than desired length.*

TOE

Rnd 1: N1: K2tog, knit to last 3 sts, k2tog, k1; N2: knit; N3: k1, ssk, knit to end—58 sts distributed as 14-29-15.

Rnd 2: Knit.

Rnd 3: N1: Knit to last 3 sts, k2tog, k1; N2: k1, ssk, knit to last 3 sts, k2tog, k1; N3: k1, ssk, knit to end—54 sts.

Rep [Rnds 2 and 3] 9 times, then with N3, knit to end of N1—18 sts distributed 9-9.

Break yarn leaving a 12" [30.5cm] tail.

With tapestry needle and tail, graft toe closed using Kitchener st.

FINISHING

Weave in all ends.

Block with steam iron.

Stitch Key
□ Knit
⊟ Purl
Tw2R

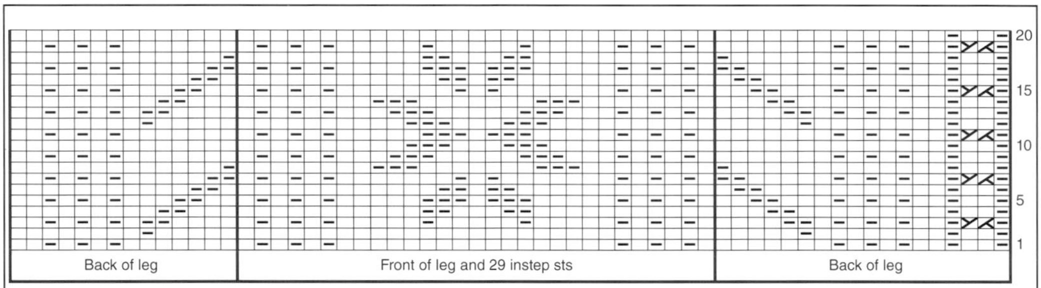

20
15
10
5
1
Back of leg
Front of leg and 29 instep sts
Back of leg

GANSEY PATTERN

CHANNEL ISLAND CAST-ON

This technique forms two stitches at once. Two strands of yarn are used together to wind around the thumb forming the bead, while a third strand is used to form the stitches. You can use both ends of one skein plus one end from a piece broken off from your ball (about 60" [152cm] long).

Holding three yarns together as one, make a slip knot 6" [15cm] from the end.

The slip knot itself is made of three loops, being formed from three strands of yarn held as one. When working this method, do not count the slip knot–you can remove and pull out that first stitch after the first round has been worked without harm to the rest of your stitches.

1. *Hold the single yarn over your left forefinger and wrap the other two yarns twice around your left thumb in a counter-clockwise direction. Your needle is in your right hand.

2. Bring the needle over, behind, and under the single yarn, just like a yarn over. (This forms the first of the two stitches made.)

3. Then insert your needle up into the two loops on the thumb (this forms the bead).

4. Pick up the single yarn again as for Step 3 (this is the second stitch), pull the new stitch through the thumb loops, tension the stitch, and rep from *.

CHANNEL ISLAND CAST-ON

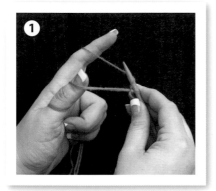

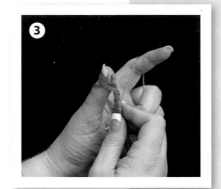

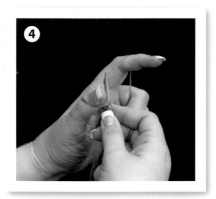

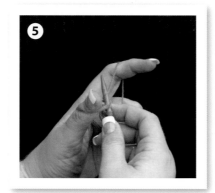

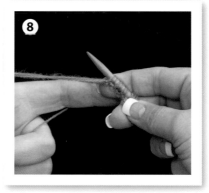

SHORT-ROW FAIR ISLE SOCKS

DESIGN BY TEVA DURHAM

Traditional Fair Isle knitting, a stranded technique in which no more than two colors are used in one row, originated on Fair Isle, one of the Shetland Islands located north of Scotland. In early Fair Isle knitting, any given color was not repeated for more than three stitches in a row to prevent long strands between colors on the back of the work. Here's a modern version of a Fair Isle sock with a twist: short rows are used to interrupt the predictable bands of color, shifting the pattern to create a diagonal band. ✍

Size
Woman's medium/large [US size 7-12]

Finished Measurements
Length from cuff to ankle: 8" [20.5cm]

Foot circumference: 9" [23cm]

Materials 🧶4
◆ Loop-d-Loop by Teva Durham Moss (DK weight; 85% extrafine merino wool/15% nylon; 163 yds [149m] per 1¾ oz [50g] ball): 2 balls Fuchsia #07 (MC); 1 ball each Brown #02 (A), Light Lilac #05 (B), and Crimson #10 (C)

◆ Size 2 [2.75mm] circular needle or size needed to obtain gauge

◆ Size 2 [2.75mm] double-pointed needles (set of 5)

◆ Size G/6 [4mm] crochet hook for trim

◆ Stitch marker

◆ Tapestry needle

Gauge
24 sts and 32 rows = 4" [10cm] in 2-color stranded St st.

Adjust needle size as necessary to obtain correct gauge.

PATTERN NOTES

- The sock is worked from cuff to toe.
- The leg is worked back and forth on a circular needle to allow for short-row patterning and for starting a row from either edge. Whenever necessary in pattern, cut yarn and slide stitches to opposite end of needle to start next row.
- After the leg is complete, stitches from the beginning and end of the leg are joined for the heel flap and heel turn. The sock is worked in the round from the gusset to the toe.
- The left and right socks have mirrored symmetry: the short rows are begun on opposite sides for each sock.
- Carry stranded yarn loosely to maintain sock's elasticity.

SPECIAL ABBREVIATIONS

W&T (Wrap and turn for short row): Bring yarn to RS of work between needles, slip next st pwise to RH needle, bring yarn around this st to WS, slip st back to LH needle, turn work to begin working back in the other direction.

Hiding wraps: On RS rows: pick up wrap from front to back and knit tog with wrapped st. On WS rows, pick up wrap from the back, then purl it tog with wrapped st. Make sure that wrap falls to WS when hiding it.

N1, N2, N3 N4: Needle 1, needle 2, needle 3, needle 4. N1 and N4 hold gusset/sole sts and N2 and N3 hold instep sts.

STITCH PATTERNS

STRIPE PATTERN

*Work 1 row A, 2 rows MC; rep from *, ending 1 row A.

COLOR PATTERNS

See Charts.

INSTRUCTIONS

FIRST SOCK

CUFF

With circular needle and A, CO 61 sts.

Beg and end with a WS row, work 7 rows in K1, P1 Rib in the Stripe pat.

LEG

Rows 1-8: Begin St st and work Chart A.

Rows 9-15: Work Stripe pat.

SHORT-ROW PATTERNING

Slide sts to other end of needle, ready to work a RS row.

Work decreasing short rows while working Chart A *(Note: Chart A begins on a RS row for this series of short rows)*:

Short-row set 1: K39, W&T; purl to end.

Short-row set 2: K33 (6 sts before last wrap), W&T; purl to end.

Short-row set 3: K27 (6 sts before last wrap), W&T; purl to end.

Short-row set 4: K21 (6 sts before last wrap), W&T; purl to end.

Cut C.

Slide sts to other end of needle, ready to work a WS row.

Next row (WS): With A, purl across all sts with A, hiding all wraps.

Next 13 rows: Work Chart B across all sts. Cut MC.

Note: The short rows make this motif appear to be slanted.

Slide sts to other end of needle, ready to work a RS row.

Next row (RS): Knit with A.

Work increasing short rows while working Chart A *(Note: Chart A begins on a WS row for this series of short rows)*:

Short-row set 1: P22, W&T; k22.

Short-row set 2: P28 sts (5 sts past wrapped st—hide the wrap as you pass it), W&T; k28.

Short-row set 3: P34 (5 sts past previous wrap (hiding wrap), W&T; k34.

Short-row set 4: P40 (5 sts past previous wrap (hiding wrap), W&T; k40.

SHAPE ANKLE

Rows 1–7: Beg and end with a WS row, work Stripe pat and *at the same time*, dec 1 st at each end on Row 4 as follows: K1, k2tog, knit to last 3 sts, ssk, k1—59 sts.

Row 8 (RS): K1 B, k2tog with B, k2 B, work Row 1 of Chart A to last 3 sts, ssk with B, k1 B—57 sts.

Rows 9–15: Cont working Chart A as est, and on pat Row 5, dec at each end once more—55 sts. Cut B and C.

Row 16: With A, knit across.

HEEL FLAP

With RS facing, slip first and last 14 sts to 1 dpn for heel flap, leaving rem 27 sts on hold on circular needle for instep.

Row 1 (WS): With another dpn and MC, purl across 28 heel sts.

Cont in St st and Stripe pat as est; work even until flap measures 2½" [6.5cm], ending with a WS row.

Cut A and cont with MC only.

TURN HEEL

Row 1 (RS): K17, ssk, k1, turn.

Row 2 (WS): Sl 1, p7, p2tog, p1, turn.

Row 3: Sl 1, k8, ssk, k1, turn.

Row 4: Sl 1, p9, p2tog, p1, turn

Cont working in this manner, working 1 more st on each row until all sts have been worked, ending with a WS row—18 sts.

GUSSET

Pick-up rnd: N1: K18 heel sts, then pick up and knit 14 sts along the left edge of flap; N2 and N3: knit across 27 instep sts; N4: pick up and knit 14 sts along right edge of flap, k9 heel sts from N1; mark beg of rnd—73 sts with 23 sts on N1, 27 instep sts on N2 and N3 combined, and 23 sts on N4.

Rnd 1: N1: Knit to last 3 sts, k2tog, k1; N2 and N3: knit; N4: k1, ssk, knit to end—71 sts.

Rnd 2: Knit.

Rep [Rnds 1 and 2] 8 more times—55 sts with 14 sts on N1, 27 sts on N2 and N3 combined, 14 sts on N4.

FOOT

Work even in est pats until foot measures approx 8" [20.5cm] from back of heel or 2" [5cm] short of desired length.

TOE

Rnd 1 (dec): N1: Knit to last 3 sts, k2tog, k1; N2: ssk, knit to end; N3: knit to last 2 sts, k2tog; N4: k1, ssk, work to end—53 sts.

Rnd 2: Knit around.

Rep [Rnds 1 and 2] 5 times, then [Rnd 1] 4 times—17 sts.

With N4, work across N1 as follows: knit to last 3 sts, k2tog, k1; transfer sts from N2 to N3—16 sts with 8 sts on each dpn.

Break yarn, leaving a 12" [30.5cm] tail.

With tapestry needle and tail, graft toe closed using Kitchener st.

FINISHING

Weave in all ends.

Block.

Sew back leg seam (the pattern will not match across short-row section).

Trim

With crochet hook and 1 strand each MC and A held together, work trim down back leg seam as follows: place slipknot on hook, ch 1, hold yarn to front of work, *insert hook through st at top of cuff, pull up a loop, ch 1; rep from *, working down to heel. Cut yarn and pull through last loop to secure. Pull ends to WS of sock and weave in.

SECOND SOCK

Work as for first sock, but reverse the short rows to create a mirror image as follows: begin first series of decreasing short rows on a WS (purl) row; begin second series of increasing short rows on a RS (knit) row.

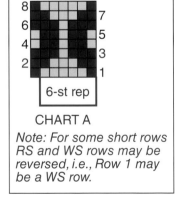

CHART A

Note: For some short rows RS and WS rows may be reversed, i.e., Row 1 may be a WS row.

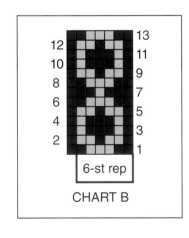

CHART B

COLOR KEY
- ■ MC
- □ B
- ■ C

SANQUHAR SOCKS

DESIGN BY BETH B. PARROTT

The unique two-colored knitting known as "Sanquhar knitting" is named for the ancient town of Sanquhar on the Nith River in the south of Scotland. This area has been known for textile production since medieval times. The knitted designs were based on older, woven patterns and evolved in the early eighteenth century. Most widely used in gloves, the best-known patterns—including "The Duke," the pattern used here—honored royalty, and those who supported the local knitting crafts.

Sanquhar socks and gloves are traditionally knit with one set of numbers in the instructions. Items are sized entirely by changing gauge by changing needle size. Traditional and modern patterns give multiple sizes using needles from size 0000 to size 3 or 4—all using fingering weight yarn. Today, we more typically use patterns with one stitch gauge and the stitch numbers change for different sizes. If there is a large pattern repeat, neither system yields a full-size range at a durable stitch gauge. This pattern has been written using a combination of both methods. ❧

Sizes
Child's medium [US size 9–10] (woman's medium [US size 8–9]/man's small [US size 7–8], man's extra large [US size 12–13 medium]) when worked in gauge specified in pattern. Instructions are given for smaller size, with larger sizes in parentheses. When only 1 number is given it applies to all sizes. See Pattern Notes, page 62 for more sizing options.

Finished Measurements
Circumference: 6 3/8" (8½, 10 5/8)" [16 (21.5, 27)cm]

Materials ①
- Jamieson's *Shetland Spindrift 2-ply* (jumper weight; 100% pure Shetland wool; 115 yds [105m] per 7/8 oz [25g] ball):

2 (2, 3) balls each Shetland Black #101 (A) and Natural White #104 (B)

- Size 1 [2.25mm] double-pointed needles (set of 5) or size needed to obtain gauge
- Stitch marker or coilless safety pin
- Tapestry needle

Gauge
41 sts and 41 rnds = 4" [10cm] in stranded 2-color St st.

Adjust needle size as necessary to obtain correct gauge.

PATTERN NOTES

- This sock is worked from the cuff down, with heel flap, gusset, and wedge toe.
- When working the leg, N1 and N2 hold front of leg stitches and N3 and N4 hold back of leg stitches; keeping the beginning of the round at the inside of the leg obscures the pattern "jog."
- When working the foot, N1 and N4 hold the sole stitches and N2 and N3 hold the instep stitches.
- 2-color stranded knitting is considerably less elastic than knitting with a single strand. It is extremely important to select the size carefully, measure gauge accurately, and adjust needle sizes appropriately to ensure proper fit.

For additional sizes, change gauge by changing needle sizes as follows:

Child's small [US size 7-8] (woman's small [US size 6–7], man's large [US size 11–12])

Circumference: 6 (8, 10)" [15 (20.5, 25.5)cm]

Gauge: 44 sts and 44 rnds = 4" [10cm].

Needles: Size 0 [2mm] or size needed to obtain gauge

Yarn: 2 balls each A and B

Child's large [US size 12-13] (woman's large [US size 10-11]/man's medium [US size 9-10], man's extra large wide [US size 13-14 wide])

Circumference: 7 (9¼, 11½)" [18 (23.5, 29)cm]

Gauge: 38 sts and 38 rnds = 4" [10cm].

Needles: Size 2 [2.75mm] or size needed to obtain gauge

Yarn: 2 (3, 3) balls each A and B

SPECIAL ABBREVIATION

N1, N2, N3, N4: Needle 1, needle 2, needle 3, needle 4.

STITCH PATTERNS

RIB (MULTIPLE OF 5 STS)

See Chart 1, page 64.

IDENTITY PANEL (30-ST PANEL)

Using Charts 2 and 3 as examples and copies of Chart 4 (blank) to work on, chart the initials and/or numbers that you will use; refer to the charted alphabet and numbers. *Be sure to chart and work them upside down so they will be right side up on your sock.*

SPOT PATTERN FOR IDENTITY PANEL AND SOLE

Rnd 1: *K1 A, k1 B, rep from *.

Rnd 2: *K1 B, k1 A, rep from *.

Rep Rnds 1 and 2 for pat.

SPOT PATTERN FOR HEEL FLAP AND HEEL TURN (ODD NUMBER OF STS)

Note: The ending slip sts form an A chain on each heel flap edge.

Row 1 (WS): *P1 A, p1 B, rep from * across to last st, sl 1 A.

Row 2: *K1 A, k1 B, rep from * across to last st, sl 1 A.

Rep Rows 1 and 2 for pat.

SANQUHAR "THE DUKE" PATTERN

See Chart 5, page 65.

INSTRUCTIONS

CUFF

With A, CO 70 (90, 110) sts. Distribute sts among 4 dpns as follows: 15-20-15-20 (20-25-20-25, 25-30-25-30). Mark beg of rnd and join, being careful not to twist sts.

Work Rnds 1–10 of Chart 1, then rep [Rnds 5–10] 0 (1, 2) times more.

Next rnd: Knit with A and dec 4 (2, 0) sts evenly around—66 (88, 110) sts.

Rearrange sts as follows: 11-22-11-22 (22-22-22-22, 22-33-22-33).

Next rnd: Knit with A.

IDENTITY PANEL

Rnd 1: Center Identity Panel as follows: N1 and N2: work 1 (7, 12) sts in Spot pat; work Row 1 of your Chart 4; work 2 (7, 13) sts in Spot pat to end of N2, continuing where you left off before panel; N3 and N4: cont in est Spot pat to end of rnd.

Rnds 2–11: Cont as established, working Chart 4 centered on N1 and N2 and Spot pat on rem sts.

LEG

Note: Adjust number of reps as desired for shorter or longer leg.

Work [Rnds 1–22 of Chart 5] 1 (2, 2) times.

Work [Rnds 1–11] 1 (0, 1) times.

Work Rnds 12 and 13 (Rnds 1 and 2; Rnds 12 and 13) once more.

HEEL FLAP

Slip sts from N3 to N4 for heel—33 (44, 55) sts on N4; sts on N1 and N2 are instep sts and rem unworked.

Turn work.

Beg with WS row and ending with a RS row, work Spot pat for 20 (28, 36) rows.

TURN HEEL

Note: Maintain est Spot pat throughout.

Row 1: P18 (24, 29), p2tog, p1; turn.

Row 2: Sl 1, k4 (5, 4), ssk, k1; turn.

Row 3: Sl 1, purl to 1 st before gap, p2tog, p1; turn.

Row 4: Sl 1, knit to 1 st before gap, ssk, k1; turn.

Rep Rows 3 and 4 until all side stitches are consumed, ending with a RS row—19 (24, 29) sts rem.

GUSSET

Note: Gusset and sole sts (N1 and N4) are worked in Spot pat throughout; instep sts (N2 and N3) are worked in Duke pat. For Gusset and Foot, when working "single-color A" rnds of Duke pat (i.e., Rnds 1, 2, 13, 14) across instep sts, carry B on WS and weave it in every 3–5 sts.

Pick-up rnd: With dpn holding heel sts (N1) and continuing in est Spot pat, pick up and knit 16 (21, 27) stitches along side of heel flap and 2 sts in gusset corner; N2 and N3: cont est Duke pat across 33 (44, 55) instep sts; N4: working in Spot pat, pick up and knit 2 sts sts in gusset corner, then 16 (21, 27) sts along side of flap, k10 (12, 15) heel sts from N1—88 (114, 142) sts with sts distributed as follows: 27-22-11-28 (35-22-22-35, 43-33-22-44).

Rnd 1 (dec): N1: Maintaining Spot pat, knit to last 2 sts, ssk with A; N2 and N3: work in est Duke pat; N4: k2tog with A, knit to end, maintaining Spot pat—86 (112, 140) sts.

Rnd 2 (dec): N1: Knit to last 3 sts, k2tog, k1 A; N2 and N3: work in est pat; N4: k1 A, ssk, knit to end—84 (110, 138) sts.

Rnd 3: Work in pat around, maintaining last st of N1 and first st of N4 in A.

Rep [Rnds 2 and 3] 9 (11, 14) times—66 (88, 110) sts.

FOOT

Work even in est pats until foot measures approx 1½ (2¼, 3)" [4 (5.5, 7.5)cm] short of desired foot length, ending with Rnd 2 or Rnd 13 of Duke pat on instep; alternatively, knit 2 rnds A as final 2 rnds.

TOE

Work in Spot Pattern on all needles, maintaining 2 sts at each side in A as established.

Rnd 1 (dec): N1: Knit to last 3 sts, k2tog, k1 A; N2: k1 A, ssk, knit to end; N3: knit to last 3 sts, k2tog, k1 A; N4: k1 A, ssk, knit to end—62 (84, 106) sts.

Rnd 2: Knit around, maintaining last st of N1 and N3 and first st of N2 and N4 in A.

Maintaining Spot pat, rep [Rnds 1 and 2] 6 (9, 12) times, then work Rnd 1 once more—34 (44, 54) sts remain.

Next rnd: N1: Work in est pat; N2, N3, N4: with A only, knit to end of rnd.

With N4 and A, knit across N1. Slip sts from N2 to N3—17 (22, 27) sts on N3 and N4.

With A, graft sts on N3 and N4 using Kitchener stitch.

Weave in ends. Block.

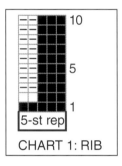

CHART 1: RIB

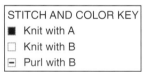

STITCH AND COLOR KEY
- ■ Knit with A
- □ Knit with B
- ⊟ Purl with B

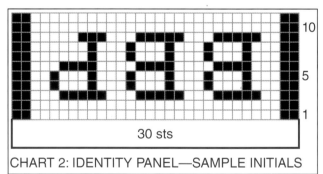

30 sts

CHART 2: IDENTITY PANEL—SAMPLE INITIALS

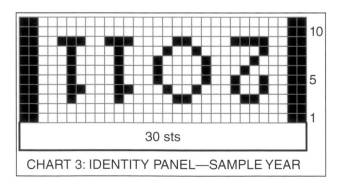

30 sts

CHART 3: IDENTITY PANEL—SAMPLE YEAR

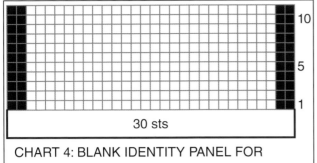

CHART 4: BLANK IDENTITY PANEL FOR
INITIALS OR NUMBERS

30 sts

CHART 5: THE "DUKE" PATTERN

22-st rep

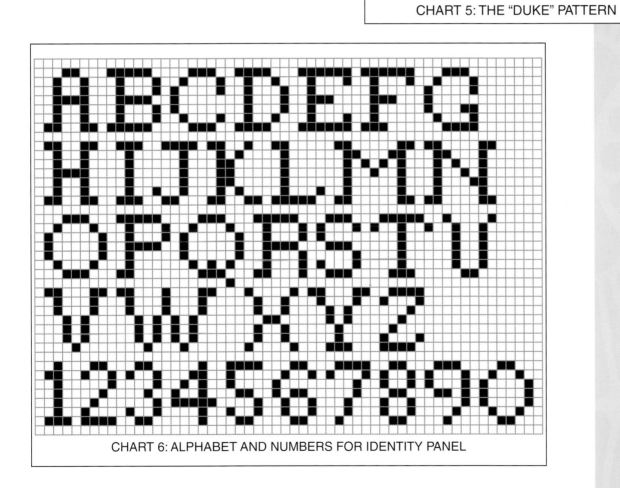

CHART 6: ALPHABET AND NUMBERS FOR IDENTITY PANEL

HE' MO LEANAN KILT HOSE

DESIGN BY ANNE CARROL GILMOUR

He' mo Leanan is the name of a favorite *orain luadh* (waulking song) it means: "Hey my Love!" in Gaelic, and is was one of the first waulking songs I ever learned to sing in this beautiful language. I designed these kilt hose for my husband, adapting the knot on our wedding bands for the cuffs and central motif, so I thought the title of this song would be an appropriate name for the pattern. ✍

Sizes

Man's medium [US size 10½–13] (large [US size 14–15]). Instructions are given for smaller size, with larger size in parentheses. When only 1 number is given, it applies to both sizes.

Finished Measurements

Cuff-to-flap length: 13 (14½)" [33 (37)cm]

Calf circumference: 12 (13½)" [30.5 (34.5)cm]

Foot circumference: 9½ (11)" [24 (28)cm]

Materials (1) Or (3)

◆ Wendy *Guernsey 5-ply* (fingering weight; 100 percent wool; 245 yds [224m] per 3½ oz [100g] ball): 3 (4) balls Natural #500

◆ Froelich *Sedrun* (DK weight; 90% wool/10% nylon; 132 yds [120m] per 1¾ oz [50g] ball): 6 balls Dark Green # 5566

◆ Size 1 (2) [2.25 (2.75)mm)] double-pointed needles (set of 4)

◆ Size 2 (3) [2.75 (3.25)mm) double-pointed needles (set of 4) or size needed to obtain gauge

◆ Size D/3 [3.25mm] crochet hook

◆ 6 stitch markers, 1 in CC for beg of rnd

◆ Tapestry needle

Gauge

26 (24) sts and 32 (30) rnds = 4" (10cm) in St st with fingering (DK) yarn and size 2 (3) needles.

Adjust needle size as necessary to obtain correct gauge.

PATTERN NOTES

- This sock is worked from cuff to toe. The cuff border is worked flat, then grafted into a ring; picot hems/edges are worked on both sides of the turned-down cuff, after which the sock is worked to the toe, with the leg shaped with a calf gusset, heel flap and heel gusset, and wedge toe.

- The sample socks worked in the green DK-weight yarn used the medium instructions; the sample socks worked with the cream hard-spun Guernsey yarn used the large instructions. You can vary the sizes by working the medium size with Guernsey yarn or the large size with DK yarn. For women's sizes, use a fingering-weight sock yarn with a denser gauge than the Guernsey yarn and follow medium instructions.

- This pattern gives you multiple pattern options for back leg cables and side "knit/purl" panels. You never have to knit the same pair twice!

SPECIAL TECHNIQUES

Provisional Cast-On: With crochet hook and waste yarn, make a chain several sts longer than desired cast-on. With knitting needle and project yarn, pick up indicated number of sts in the "bumps" on back of chain. When indicated in pattern, "unzip" the crochet chain to free live sts.

Nupp: Bring RH needle from front to back between second and third sts on LH needle; wrap yarn around RH needle, draw it through, then place loop on end of LH needle. K1 in loop just made, slip the 2 wrapped to RH needle, then pass the third st on RH needle over the 2 wrapped sts.

To keep the hem from twisting, slide an empty dpn under the cuff sts (do this one dpn at a time). Use a third dpn to do the bind-off, as in a standard 3-needle bind-off. I like to use a larger dpn for the third needle, to keep the bind-off from becoming too tight.

INSTRUCTIONS

CUFF

Cuff Border

Using provisional method and larger dpn, CO 15 sts.

With larger dpns and working back and forth, work 4 reps of Cuff Chart.

Unzip waste yarn of provisional CO; graft live sts to live CO sts to form a ring.

Turned Picot Hem

Bottom of cuff when it's turned down

With larger dpns, pick up (but don't knit) under all the purl bumps around the ring; mark beg of rnd—56 (60) sts on dpns.

Rnd 1: Knit and inc 12 (16) sts evenly around—68 (76) sts.

Rnds 2–5: Work in garter st (knit 1 rnd, purl 1 rnd).

Rnds 6–8: Knit.

Rnd 9 (picot turning rnd): [Yo, k2tog] around.

Rnds 10–12 (hem): Knit.

Bind-off rnd: Turn the hem edge up behind your cuff with purl sides together (it will fold nicely along the line of picot stitches); carefully catch the first hem st with its corresponding cuff st and knit these 2 sts tog; *knit the next hem st tog with the next cuff st; BO 1 st very loosely; rep from * around. *Notes: Try not to pull your working yarn too tightly while binding off to maintain elasticity of cuff. Make sure you continue working stitch for stitch—if you off-set any of the sts your hem will twist in an unattractive manner.*

Turned Picot Cuff Top

Work 12 rnds as for Turned Picot Hem.

Joining rnd: Turn the edge up behind your cuff with purl sides together as before; carefully catch the first live st with its corresponding cuff st and knit these 2 sts tog; *knit the next live st tog with the next cuff st; rep from * around. *Do not bind off*—68 (76) sts rem.

Ribbed Garter

Switch to smaller dpns.

Work 23 rnds in K2, P2 Rib for sock "garter."

Reverse Cuff

With yarn at back, slip first st to the RH needle. Bring yarn forward and transfer st back to LH needle, then turn the work as if you were knitting flat. Flip the entire cuff inside-out through the ring formed by your dpns so that you can work in the opposite direction—you have, in effect, made a wrapped st "U-turn," so that when the cuff is folded down as worn, the RS of the work will show.

LEG

Leg has 6 panels around: Calf Chart, Back Leg Cable of choice, K/P pat A of choice, Center Knot pat, K/P pat B of choice, Back Leg Cable of choice. 1 st is slipped between each panel every other rnd.

Set-up rnd: Switch to larger dpns; sl 1, p19, sl 1, pm; p1 (2), [k1, M1] 4 times, k1, M1p, p0 (1), pm; sl 1, p1 (2), k6, p1 (2), pm; work Rnd 1 of Center Front Knot Chart over the next 17 sts (center front leg), pm; p1 (2), k6, p1 (2), sl 1, pm; p1 (2), [k1, M1] 4 times, k1, M1p, p0 (1); mark beg of rnd—78 (86) sts. *Note: This rnd counts as Rnd 1 of all leg pattern charts.*

Rnd 2: Working Rnd 2 of each chart, work Calf Chart over 21 sts to first marker, sm; work Back Leg Cable Chart of choice over 11 (13) sts, sm; work K/P Chart A of choice over 9 (11) sts, sm; work Center Knot Chart over 17 sts, sm; work K/P Chart B of choice over 9 (11) sts, sm; work Back Leg Cable Chart of your choice over 11 (13) sts.

Work in est pats until Calf Chart is complete—1 st rem for Calf. On following rnds, work that st as: sl 1 on odd rnds and k1-tbl on even rnds—62 (70) sts.

Cont in est pats until Center Knot Chart is complete, then work even, purling all sts between slipped sts of Center Knot Panel, until sock reaches desired length to heel flap—54 (62) sts.

DIVIDE FOR HEEL FLAP

Change to smaller dpns for remainder of sock.

With smaller dpn, k14 (16) sts; keep 27 (31) center front sts on hold for instep; transfer rem 13 (15) back leg sts to first dpn for heel flap—27 (31) heel flap sts.

HEEL FLAP

Row 1 (WS): K1, yf, *sl 1, p1; rep from * to last 2 sts, sl 1; yb, k1.

Row 2 (RS): Knit across.

Rep [Rows 1 and 2] 12 (13) times—26 (28) rows.

TURN HEEL

Row 1 (WS): K1, yf, [sl 1, p1] 7 (8) times, p2tog, p1; turn. 9, 11

Row 2 (RS): Sl 1, k4, ssk, k1; turn.

Row 3: [Sl 1, p1] 3 times, p2tog, p1; turn. 7, 9

Row 4: Sl 1, k6, ssk, k1; turn.

Row 5: Sl 1, p2, [sl 1, p1] twice, sl 1, p2tog, p1; turn. 5, 7

Row 6: Sl 1, k8, ssk, k1; turn.

Row 7: [Sl 1, p1] 5 times, p2tog, p1; turn. 3, 5

Row 8: Sl 1, k10, ssk, k1; turn.

Row 9: Sl 1, p2, [sl 1, p1] 4 times, sl 1, p2tog, p1; turn. 1, 3

Row 10: Sl 1, k12, ssk, k1, turn.

Row 11: [Sl 1, p1] 7 times, p2tog, p0 (1); turn.

Row 12: Sl 1, k13 (14), ssk, k0 (1); turn for large.

Medium heel is complete; do not turn—15 sts.

Large only

Row 13: Sl 1, p2, [sl 1, p1] 6 times, sl 1, p2tog; turn.

Row 14: Sl 1, k15, ssk; do not turn—17 sts.

HEEL GUSSET

Note: When working K/P pat on instep, complete last pat rep from leg (if necessary), then work Rnd 1 only of chart to toe shaping.

Set-up rnd: N1: With dpn holding heel sts, pick up and knit into first 12 (13) garter bumps along side of heel flap, then pick up and *purl* into last bump; N2 (instep sts): work in est pat as follows: maintaining slip-st chains between panels, work K/P pat; p11 sts from Center Front Panel; work K/P pat; N3: pick up and purl into first garter bump of heel flap, then pick up and knit into rem 12 (13) bumps; k7 (8) heel sts from N1—68 (76) sts with 21 (23) sts on N1; 27 (31) sts on N2; and 20 (22) sts on N3.

Rnd 1 (dec): N1: Knit to last 3 sts, k2tog, p1; N2: work as est; N3: p1, ssk, knit to end—66 (74) sts.

Rnd 2: N1: Knit to last st, p1; N2: work as est; N3: p1, knit to end.

Rep [Rnds 1 and 2] 6 times—54 (62) sts.

Next rnd: N1: Knit to last 3 sts, k2tog, p1; N2 and N3: work as est—53 (61) sts with 13 (15) sts each on N1 and N3 and 27 (31) sts on N2.

FOOT

Work even in est pats until foot measures approx 2 (2½)" [5 (6.5)cm] short of desired length.

TOE

Dec rnd: N1: Knit to last 3 sts, k2tog, k1; N2: k1, ssk, knit to last 3 sts, k2tog, k1; N3: ssk, knit to end—49 (57) sts.

Rnd 2: N1: *K1, sl 1; rep from * to last 3 sts, k3; N2: k2, *k1, sl 1; rep from * to last 3 sts, k3; N3: K2, *k1, sl 1; rep from * end.

Rep Dec rnd [every other rnd] 8 (10) times, maintaining est heel-st pat on even rnds.

FINISHING

Break yarn leaving a 18" [46cm] tail. With tapestry needle and tail, graft toe closed using Kitchener st. Wet block socks to finished measurements.

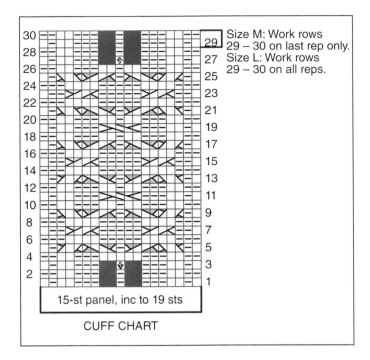

Size M: Work rows
29 – 30 on last rep only.
Size L: Work rows
29 – 30 on all reps.

15-st panel, inc to 19 sts

CUFF CHART

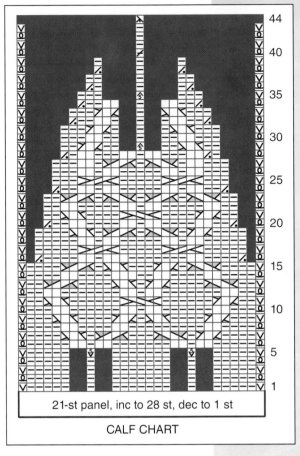

21-st panel, inc to 28 st, dec to 1 st

CALF CHART

STITCH KEY

⊟	Purl on RS, knit on WS
☐	Knit on RS, purl on WS
■	No stitch
☑	Sl 1 purlwise
🔟	K1-tbl
⬇	Inc 1-to-5: See Special Techniques
⬆	Yb, sl 3, k2tog-tbl, pass 3 slipped sts over
◪	P2tog
⬇	Wyib, sl 2, yf, p1, pass 2 slipped sts over
⬇	Wyib, sl 1 kwise, k2tog-tbl, psso
⊟⊟	Nupp: See Special Techniques
	Sl 1 to cn and hold in back, k2, p1 from cn
	Sl 2 to cn an hold in front, p1, k2 from cn
	Sl 2 to cn and hold in back, k2, k2 from cn
	Sl 2 to cn and hold in front, k2, k2 from cn
	Sl 2 to cn and hold in back, k2, p2 from cn
	Sl 2 to ch and hold in front, p2, k2 from cn
	Sl 3 to cn and hold in back, k2, slip purl st back to LH needle and p1, k2 from cn
	Sl 3 to cn and hold in front, k2, slip purl st back to LH needle and p1, k2 from cn

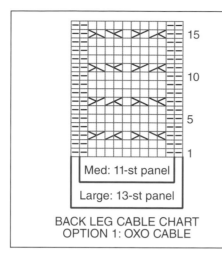

BACK LEG CABLE CHART
OPTION 1: OXO CABLE

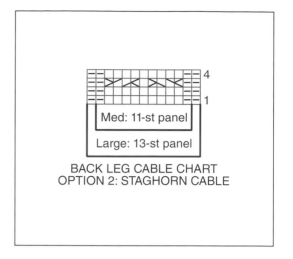

BACK LEG CABLE CHART
OPTION 2: STAGHORN CABLE

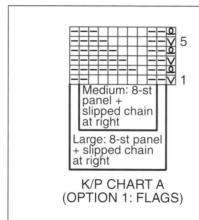

K/P CHART A
(OPTION 1: FLAGS)

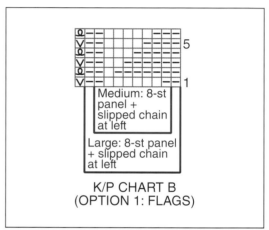

K/P CHART B
(OPTION 1: FLAGS)

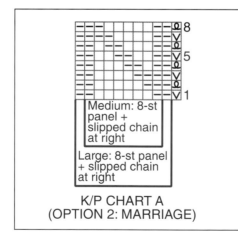

K/P CHART A
(OPTION 2: MARRIAGE)

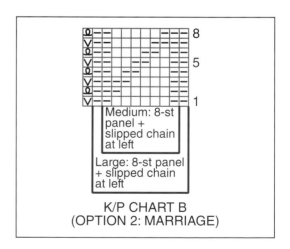

K/P CHART B
(OPTION 2: MARRIAGE)

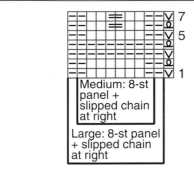

**K/P CHART A
(OPTION 3: NUPPS & LADDERS)**

Note: This pattern is worked over an odd number of rnds. Maintain slipped chain every other rnd.

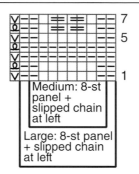

**K/P CHART B
(OPTION 3: NUPPS & LADDERS)**

Note: This pattern is worked over an odd number of rnds. Maintain slipped chain every other rnd.

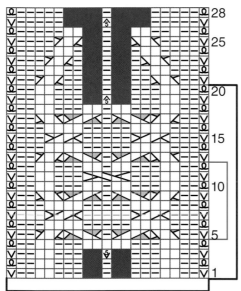

17-st panel, inc to 21 sts, dec to 13 sts

CENTER FRONT KNOT CHART

NOTES

Work 3 reps of Rows 1– 20.

First Rep: Work Rows 5 – 12 twice for double-knot. (total: 28 rnds)

2nd Rep: Work Rows 5 – 12 3 times for triple-knot. (total: 36 rnds)

3rd Rep: Work Rows 5 – 12 twice for double-knot. (total: 28 rnds)

To make leg shorter, work Rows 5 – 12 twice on 2nd rep.

To make leg longer, work [Rows 5 – 12] 3 times on First or 2nd Rep, or both.

After 3 reps are complete, work Rows 21 – 28, then work row 28 only until leg is desired length to heel.

SOCKS OF EUROPE

ESTONIAN KIHNU SOCK

DESIGN BY NANCY BUSH

The inspiration for these ethnic socks comes from those worn by the women of Kihnu Island, a small island in the Baltic Sea, off the coast of Estonia. Knitting has been a major craft on Kihnu for hundreds of years. The women wear long, over the knee, hand-knit stockings with their colorful, handwoven striped skirts. The long stockings have colorful patterns at the knee, which can usually be seen when the women walk or dance. Still worn today, these stockings are knit by young girls for their dowries; pairs of them are given to their new mothers-in-law.

These short socks carry similar patterns to their longer counterparts. The main pattern is worked in red, white, and blue yarn. Traditionally, the white was natural sheep's wool, the red was dyed with madder, and the blue was colored with indigo or woad (known as "pot blue"). Madder was prized on Kihnu beyond its lovely color, as it was thought that madder offered protection against plague. Most knitted items (socks, mittens, even men's sweaters) had red near the openings to protect the wearer.

Size
Woman's medium [US size 8–9]

Finished Measurements
Length from cuff to ankle: 8" [20.5cm]

Foot circumference: 8" [20.5cm]

Materials 1
◆ Elemental Effects *Shetland Fingering* (fingering weight; 100% American Shetland wool; 118 yds [108m] per 1 oz [28g] skein): Three skeins White (MC); 1 skein each Midnight Blue (A) and Scarlet (B)

◆ Size 1 [2.25mm] double-pointed needles (set of 5) or size needed to obtain gauge

◆ Tapestry needle

Gauge
◆ 32 sts and 40 rnds = 4" [10cm] in St st (before blocking).

◆ *Adjust needle size as necessary to obtain correct gauge.*

PATTERN NOTES
- This sock is worked from the cuff down with with flap, Dutch heel and star toe.
- There is a left and a right sock. When working the leg, rounds begin at the side instead of the back of leg so that the color changes occur at the inside of each leg.

SPECIAL ABBREVIATIONS
LC (Left Cross): Knit into back of second st, knit into front of first st, then slip both sts off needle.

RC (Right Cross): K2tog, don't drop off, knit into first st again and slip both sts off needle.

SPECIAL TECHNIQUE
Cross-Over Join: Join cast-on sts into a round as follows: slip the first cast-on st (at the point of the LH needle) onto the RH needle. With the LH needle, pick up the last cast-on st (which is now 1 st in from the end of the RH needle) and bring it up over the top of the previously moved st, placing it onto the point of the LH needle. In essence, the first and last cast-on sts have changed places and the last cast-on st surrounds the first.

The large pattern is made up of two parts, *surr lapp* (big patch) and *vahelapp* (intermediate patch). The big patch contains the central pattern with the eight-pointed star figure and the intermediate patch is the X pattern between.

Another feature is the *sukahambad* or "teeth" of the sock pattern. This is the few rows of blue and white that border the lower edge of the larger pattern. Extending below the tooth pattern is the *vikeldused* or textured pattern, usually made of traveling stitches or knit and purl patterns that run down the leg and the sides of the heel flap.

Information for this design comes from *Elemõnu*, by Rosaali Karjam, text translated by Maret Tamjärv, with many thanks. ☙

STITCH PATTERNS

OPENWORK (10-ST REP)
Rnd 1: K1, yo, k3, sk2p, k3, yo; rep from * around.

Rnd 2: Knit around.

Rep Rnds 1 and 2 for pat.

COLOR PATTERNS
See Charts.

LOWER LEG/INSTEP AND HEEL PATTERNS
See Charts.

INSTRUCTIONS

CUFF
With two needles held parallel and using a long-tail method and MC, CO 70 sts. Distribute sts evenly on 4 dpns; mark beg of rnd and join with a Cross-Over Join, taking care not to twist sts.

Rnds 1–4: [Purl 1 rnd, knit 1 rnd] twice.

Rnds 5–10: Work 6 rnds of Openwork pat.

Rnds 11 and 12: Purl 1 rnd, knit 1 rnd.

Rnd 13: Purl 1 rnd and dec 2 sts evenly around—68 sts with 17 sts on each dpn.

UPPER LEG

Rnd 1: With A, knit 1 rnd.

Rnd 2: With MC, knit 1 rnd.

Rnd 3: With A and B, *k2 A, k2 B; rep from * around.

Rnd 4: With MC, knit 1 rnd.

Rnd 5: With A, knit 1 rnd.

Next 23 rnds: Work Main Chart.

Next 5 rnds: Rep Rnds 1–5 and on last rnd, dec 4 sts evenly around—64 sts with 16 sts on each dpn.

Next 5 rnds: Work Tooth pat following chart.

Next rnd: With MC, knit 1 rnd.

LOWER LEG (LEFT SOCK)

Rnd 1 (set-up pat): N1 and N2 (front leg/instep sts): P1, LC, k3, p1, k18, p1, k3, RC, p1; N3 and N4 (back leg/heel sts): p1, k1-tbl, p1, k1-tbl, p1, k22, p1, k1-tbl, p1, k1-tbl, p1.

Rnds 2–27: Cont following Left Leg charts.

Rnd 28: N1 and N2: Work 32 instep sts as est; N3: [k1, p1] in first st, work as est to end; N4: work as est to last st, [p1, k1] in last st, turn—66 sts with 34 heel sts.

LOWER LEG (RIGHT SOCK)

Rnd 1 (set-up pat): N1 and N2 (back leg/heel sts): P1, k1-tbl, p1, k1-tbl, p1, k22, p1, k1-tbl, p1, k1-tbl, p1; N3 and N4 (front leg/instep sts): p1, LC, k3, p1, k18, p1, k3, RC, p1.

Rnds 2–27: Cont following Right Leg charts.

Rnd 28: N1: [K1, p1] in next st, work as est to end; N2: work as est to last st, [p1, k1] in last st, turn; N3 and N4: leave unworked for instep—66 sts with 34 heel sts.

HEEL FLAP

Row (WS): *Sl 1, work heel pat as est across 32 sts, p1.

Row 2 (RS): Sl 1, work heel pat as est across 32 sts, k1.

Work 30 more rows in est heel pat, slipping first st of every row, purling last st of every WS row and knitting last st of every RS row.

TURN HEEL

Row 1 (WS): Sl 1, p20, p2tog, leaving rem sts unworked.

Row 2: Sl 1, k8, ssk.

Row 3: Sl 1, p8, p2tog.

Rep Rows 2 and 3 until all side sts are in work, ending with a RS row—10 sts rem..

GUSSET

Note: Pick up into the back half of the chain st at the edge of the heel flap. This will make a "line" between the heel flap and the picked-up gusset sts.

Pick-up rnd: With needle holding heel sts (now N1), pick up and knit 16 sts along side of heel flap; N2 and N3: work across 32 instep sts, maintaining est pat; N4: pick up and knit 16 sts along side of heel flap, then knit 5 heel sts from N1; mark beg of rnd—74 sts with 21 sts each on N1 and N4 and 16 sts each on N2 and N3.

Rnd 2: N1: Knit to last 3 sts, k2tog, k1; N2 and N3: work instep pats as est; N4: k1, ssk, knit to end—72 sts.

Rnd 3: Work even, maintaining instep pat.

Rep [Rnds 2 and 3] 4 times—64 sts with 16 sts on each dpn.

FOOT

Work even, maintaining instep pat, until foot measures 7½" [19cm] or 2¼" [6cm] short of desired finished length.

TOE

Rnd 1: *K6, k2tog; rep from * around—56 sts. Knit 6 rnds.

Rnd 8: *K5, k2tog; rep from * around—48 sts. Knit 5 rnds.

Rnd 14: *K4, k2tog; rep from * around—40 sts. Knit 4 rnds.

Rnd 19: *K3, k2tog; rep from *around—32 sts. Knit 3 rnds.

Rnd 23: *K2, k2tog; rep from * around—24 sts. Knit 2 rnds.

Rnd 26: *K1, k2tog; rep from * around—16 sts. Knit 1 rnd.

Rnd 28: K2tog around—8 sts.

FINISHING

Break yarn, leaving a 6" [15cm] tail. Using tapestry needle, thread tail through rem sts, and pull tight. Weave in all ends. Wash gently and block on sock blockers or under a damp towel.

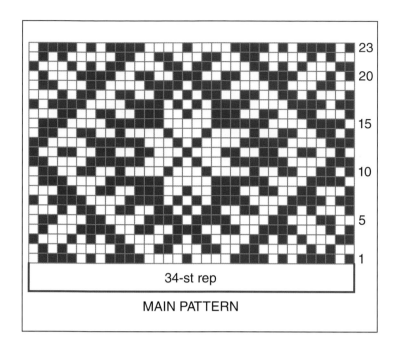

34-st rep

MAIN PATTERN

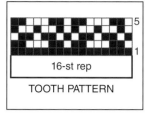

16-st rep

TOOTH PATTERN

COLOR AND STITCH KEY

☐ MC
■ A
■ B
⊟ P on RS, k on WS
▣ K1-tbl on RS, p1-tbl on WS
☐ Knit
▧ RC
▨ LC

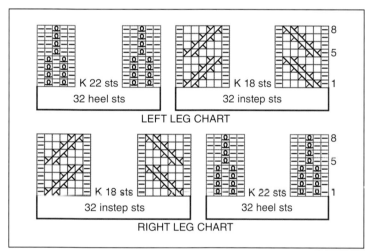

K 22 sts

32 heel sts

K 18 sts

32 instep sts

LEFT LEG CHART

K 18 sts

32 instep sts

K 22 sts

32 heel sts

RIGHT LEG CHART

ESTONIAN KAPÕTAD SOCKS

DESIGN BY NANCY BUSH

Kapõtad in the Kihnu dialect is a word for men's socks. *Kapõtad* came in either stripes or a single color. Men wore white socks for festival days and black or gray socks for work. Striped socks were a later fashion, worn for festival times rather than work. Women would knit *dapõtad* using stripe designs of their own choosing. Sometimes they would add a symbol or figure under the heel (it could be a family or farm mark) to indicate who owned the sock if it was lost. Today this style of sock is popular on Kihnu and is even worn by women.

I designed my own *kapõtad*, drawing from elements of several I have seen. I added a small eight-pointed star under the heel, to carry on the Kihnu tradition.

Information for this design comes from *Elemõnu*, by Rosaali Karjam, text translated by Maret Tamjärv, with many thanks. ᴥ

Size
Woman's medium [US size 8-9]

Finished Measurements
Length from cuff to ankle: 8" [20.5cm]

Foot circumference: 8" [20.5cm]

Materials 🧶**1**
◆ Helmi Vuorelma Oy (from Finland) Satakieli (fingering weight; 100% wool; 360 yds [3290m] per 3½ oz [100g]

skein): 1 skein Grey #901 (MC); ½ skein each Purple #582 (A), Blue #966 (B), Moss Green #985 (C), and Rust #288 (D)

◆ Size 0 [2mm] double-pointed needles (set of 5) or size needed to obtain gauge

◆ Stitch marker

◆ Tapestry needle

Gauge
36 sts and 48 rnds = 4" [10cm] in St st (before blocking).

Adjust needle size as necessary to obtain correct gauge.

PATTERN NOTES

◆ This sock is worked from the cuff down; there is a band of stripes on the heel flap and a star on the square heel turn; the toe is a pointed wedge toe.

◆ This pattern is worked so there is a left and a right sock. Rounds begin at the inside instead of the back of leg so that the color changes occur at the inside of each leg.

SPECIAL TECHNIQUE

Cross-Over Join: Join cast-on sts into a round as follows: slip the first cast-on st (at the point of the LH needle) onto the RH needle. With the LH needle, pick up the last cast-on st (which is now 1 st in from the end of the RH needle) and bring it up over the top of the previously moved st, placing it onto the point of the LH needle. In essence, the first and last cast-on sts have changed places and the last cast-on st surrounds the first.

STITCH PATTERNS

STRIPE PATTERN A (7 RNDS)

Work 1 rnd each in the following order: A, MC, C, B, C, MC, A.

STRIPE PATTERN B (7 RNDS)

Work 1 rnd each in the following order: B, MC, C, A, C, MC, B.

PATTERNS C AND D, STAR MOTIF

See charts.

INSTRUCTIONS

CUFF AND LEG

With two needles held parallel and using a long-tail method and MC, CO 72 sts. Distribute sts evenly on 4 dpns; mark beg of rnd and join with a Cross-Over Join, taking care not to twist sts.

Work 22 rnds in K2, P2 Rib.

Knit 3 rnds.

Rnds 1–7: Work Stripe Pat A.

Rnds 8–14: With MC, knit 7 rnds.

Rnds 15–21: Work 7 rnds Stripe Pat B.

Rnds 22–28: With MC, knit 7 rnds.

Rnds 29–35: Work 7 rnds Stripe Pat A.

Rnds 36–42: With MC, knit 7 rnds.

Rnds 43–49: Work 7 rnds Pat C.

Rnds 50–56: With MC, knit 7 rnds.

Rnds 57–64: Work 8 rnds Pat D.

HEEL FLAP (LEFT SOCK)

Note: Slip the edge sts where possible, as you add in new colors. If you find you are ready to begin a row and the color you need is on the other side, simply begin the row at the side where the color is attached, always keeping in St st.

Break MC. Slip next 37 sts onto 2 dpns to hold for instep.

Row 1 (RS): Join MC and knit across rem 35 heel sts.

Row 2: Sl 1, p34.

Row 3: Sl 1, k34.

Rep Rows 2 and 3 twice more.

Work 7 rows Stripe Pat C, slipping the edge sts where possible.

Work 20 rows St st with MC, slipping first st of each row, ending with a WS row. You should have approx 17 chains up each side of the flap.

HEEL FLAP (RIGHT SOCK)

Row 1 (RS): With MC, k35, turn. Slip rem 37 sts onto 2 dpns to hold for instep.

Beg with Row 2, complete flap as for Left Sock.

TURN HEEL

Row 1 (RS): Sl 1, k22, ssk; turn, leaving rem sts unworked.

Row 2: *Sl 1, p12, p2tog.

Row 3: Sl 1, k12, ssk.

Row 4: Sl 1, work Star Motif across next 11 sts, p2tog.

Continue working Star Motif and turning heel until all side sts are in work—13 sts.

GUSSET

Note: Pick up into the whole st as you work the sides of the heel flap, adjusting for the few rows where you might not have a slipped edge st. Read gusset instructions through because striping occurs while decreasing gusset.

Pick-up rnd: With needle holding heel sts (N1) and cont with MC, pick up and knit 17 sts along side of heel flap; N2 and N3: k37, keeping sts divided on 2 dpns; N4: pick up and knit 17 sts along side of heel flap, then k7 heel sts from N1; mark beg of rnd—84 sts with 23 sts on N1, 18 sts on N2, 19 sts on N3, and 24 sts on N4.

Rnd 2 (dec): N1: Work to last 3 sts, k2tog, k1; N2 and N3: knit across; N4: k1, ssk, knit to end—82 sts.

Rnd 3: Work even.

Rep [Rnds 2 and 3] 5 times—72 sts.

At the same time, on Rnd 8 (7 rnds of MC from Pat D on instep), beg Pat C; on Pat C Rnd 4, work 1A, *2D, 2A; rep from * around, ending with 1A.

Cont in pat, decreasing as necessary to complete gusset shaping.

FOOT

Work even in est pat, working 7 rnds MC between alternating Pats D and C, ending having completed the second Pat D on the foot.

Knit 3 rnds with MC.

TOE

Adjust sts so you have 18 sts on each dpn.

Color pattern: Dec for toe following instructions below and at the same time, work 4 rnds with MC; work Pat C, then knit with MC to end.

Rnd 1 (dec): N1: Knit to last 2 sts, k2tog; N2: ssk, knit to end; N3 and N4: work as for N1 and N2—68 sts.

Rnd 2: Knit around.

Rep [Rnds 1 and 2] 8 times—36 sts.

Rep [Rnd 1] 7 times—8 sts.

FINISHING

Break yarn, leaving a 6" [15cm] tail. Using tapestry needle, thread tail through rem sts, and pull tight. Weave in all ends. Wash gently and block on sock blockers or under a damp towel.

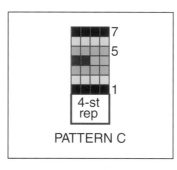

PATTERN C

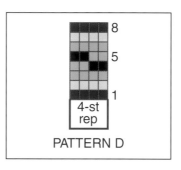

PATTERN D

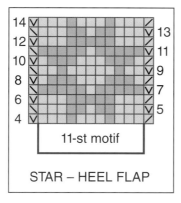

STAR – HEEL FLAP

COLOR AND STITCH KEY

☐ MC
■ A
■ B
☐ C
▨ D
☑ Sl 1
▧ P2tog on WS
◩ Ssk on RS

IDES OF MARCH SOCKS

DESIGN BY STAR ATHENA

The Ides of March was once a festive day dedicated to the Roman god Mars. In modern times, the term "the Ides of March" is best known as the date of Julius Caesar's assassination in 44 BC. This sock design, which was inspired by an ancient Roman tile, uses a technique called Mosaic knitting. Barbara Walker named the process of slipping stitches while alternating rows of color "mosaic knitting" because it naturally lends itself to geometric design. Unlike stranded knitting, you work with only one color at a time, while slipping specific stitches to give the illusion of colorwork. In this pattern, you will work two rounds of one color, slipping the stitches that are indicated as the second color, then work two rounds of the other color, slipping the stitches that are indicated as the first color. ❧

Sizes
Woman's small [US size 3–6] (medium [US size 6–9], large [US size 8–12]). Instructions are given for smallest size, with larger sizes in parentheses. When only one number is given, it applies to all sizes.

Finished Measurements
Foot circumference (unstretched): 7 (8, 9)" [17.5 (20, 23)cm]

Materials [1]
◆ Shalimar Yarns Zoe Sock (fingering weight; 100% superwash merino wool; 450 yds [411m] per 3½ oz [100g] skein): One skein Cayenne (MC)
◆ Dream in Color Smooshy (fingering weight; 100% superwash merino wool; 450 yds [411m] per 4 oz [113g] skein): One skein Purple Rain #006 (CC)
◆ Size 1 [2.25mm] needles:

◆ One 32" [80cm] circular needle (magic loop method)

Or

Two 24" [60cm] circular needles (two circular needles method)

Or

Double-pointed needles (set of 5) or size needed to obtain gauge

◆ Cable needle

◆ Size C/2 [2.75mm] crochet hook for provisional cast-on

◆ Stitch marker for beg of rnd (optional)

◆ Tapestry needle

Gauge
32 sts and 48 rnds = 4" [10cm] in St st.

Adjust needle size as necessary to obtain correct gauge.

PATTERN NOTES

- This sock pattern is worked from the cuff down with two colors. It includes a sideways cabled cuff, mosaic knitting, a heel flap, gusset, and wedge toe.

- The slipped stitches create a fabric that is slightly less stretchy than standard stockinette stitch. Keep this in mind when choosing yarn and sock size.

- This pattern is written using the Magic Loop or two-circular method, where half the stitches (heel/sole) are on Needle 1 (N1), and the other half (instep) are on Needle 2 (N2). You can easily divide these stitches again for double-pointed needles. The small and large sizes have an odd number of chart repeats, so you may find it easier to split the stitches onto your needles after four repeats. Just be sure to adjust your stitches prior to working the heel flap as instructed.

- ***What is mosaic knitting?*** Describing mosaic knitting is harder than actually doing it.

SPECIAL ABBREVIATIONS

N1, N2: Needle 1 (heel/sole sts); needle 2 (instep sts).

Special Technique

Provisional Cast-On: With crochet hook and waste yarn, make a chain several sts longer than desired cast-on. With knitting needle and project yarn, pick up indicated number of sts in the "bumps" on back of chain. When indicated in pat, "unzip" the crochet chain and place live sts on needle.

STITCH PATTERNS

See charts.

INSTRUCTIONS

CUFF

With MC and using a provisional method, CO 27 sts, leaving a 12" [31cm] tail.

Work Rows 1–8 of Cuff Chart 14 (16, 18) times.

Unzip the waste yarn from the provisional cast-on; using the tail and Kitchener st, graft live CO sts to sts on needle to form a tube. *Note: The first st of the first row was a slipped st. Be sure to graft that st (or alternatively the purl st from Row 2, if you find that more comfortable).*

LEG

With RS facing and using MC, pick up and purl 56 (64, 72) sts along slipped-stitch edge of cuff, going under both legs of each slipped stitch; this will form an edge along the bottom of the cuff where it meets the leg of the sock.

Divide sts evenly between needles and join to begin working in the round.

Set-up rnd: With MC, k42 (48, 54) sts. Mark this as beg of rnd and re-arrange sts on needles so that there are again 28 (32, 36) sts on N1 and N2.

Join CC and work Rnds 1-16 of Leg Chart (following chart for size you are working) 4 times.

To increase length, rep Leg Chart until desired length, ending after Rnd 16.

HEEL FLAP

The heel flap will be worked back and forth over the first 28 (32, 36) sts on N1; any additional sts on N1 should be transferred to N2 to be held for instep.

Work 28 (32, 36) rows following Heel Flap Chart, beg and end where indicated for size being worked.

TURN HEEL [NEED HEEL SHOT]

Worked with MC

Row 1 (RS): Sl 1, k15 (17, 19), ssk, k1; turn.

Row 2: Sl 1, p5, p2tog, p1; turn.

Row 3: Sl 1, k6, ssk, k1, turn.

Row 4: Sl 1, p7, p2tog, p1; turn.

Cont working in this manner, working 1 more st on each row until all sts have been worked, ending with a WS row. *Note: Last 2 rows will end with decs—16 (18, 20) sts.*

GUSSET

Note: In this next section, the beg of rnd will shift 1 st to the left at each color change until the beg of the rnd is just before the center of the sole. This will help conceal the jogs in the stripes when changing colors along the foot.

SET-UP RND

Medium only

N1: With CC, k8, sl 1, k9; pick up and knit 16 sts along edge of heel flap, pick up and knit 1 st between heel flap and instep, pm; N2: work Rnd 1 of Leg Chart across 32 instep sts; pm; with CC, pick up and knit 1 st between instep and heel flap, pick up and knit 16 sts along other edge of heel flap—84 sts with 35 sts on N1 and 49 sts on N2.

SMALL AND LARGE ONLY

N1: With CC, k7 (9), sl 1, k8 (10); pick up and knit 14 (18) sts along edge of heel flap, pick up and knit 1 st between heel flap and instep, pm; N2: work Rnd 1 Instep Chart across 28 (36) instep sts, pm; with CC, pick up and knit 1 st between instep and heel flap, pick up and k14 (18) sts along other edge of heel flap—74 (94) sts with 31 (39) sts on N1 and 43 (55) sts on N2.

Rnd 1 (dec): N1: With CC, k7 (8, 9), sl 1, k8 (9, 10), p13 (15, 17), k2tog; N2: following chart, work est pat between markers; ssk, p13 (15, 17), k1 from N1 (beg of rnd shifted 1 st to the left)—72 (82, 92) sts.

Rnd 2: N1: With MC, k7 (8, 9), sl 1, knit to end; N2: work est pat between markers, knit to end of rnd.

Rnd 3 (dec): N1: With MC, knit to previously slipped CC st, sl 1, knit to last 2 sts, k2tog; N2: work est pat between markers; ssk, knit to end of rnd, k1 from N1—70 (80, 90) sts.

Rnd 4: N1: With CC, knit to previously slipped MC st, sl 1, knit to end; N2: work est pat between markers; knit to end of rnd.

Rnd 5 (dec): N1: With CC, knit to previously slipped MC st, sl 1, knit to last 2 sts, k2tog; N2: work est pat between markers; ssk, knit to end of rnd, k1 from N1—68 (78, 88) sts.

Rnd 6: N1: With MC, knit to previously slipped CC st, sl 1, knit to end; N2: work est pat between markers; knit to end of rnd.

Rep [Rnds 3–6] 3 (3, 4) times, then rep [Rnds 3 and 4] 0 (1, 0) times—56 (64, 72) sts. Continue to knit 1 extra st at the end of odd rnds until the first st on N1 is the first slipped st (center of sole). The slipped st will mark beg of rnd until you reach the toe.

Rearrange sts so that there are 28 (32, 36) sts on each needle, with N1 holding sole sts and N2 holding instep sts.

FOOT

Work even, alternating 2 rnds MC, 2 rnds CC, working pat as est between markers and slipping center sole sts as est, until foot measures approx 2" [5cm] short of desired length, ending at center sole and having worked Rnd 8 or 16 of pat on instep sts.

TOE

Worked with MC

Set-up: With MC, knit to end of N1; this will be new beg of rnd, with sole sts still on N1 and instep sts on N2.

Rnd 1 (dec): N1: K1, ssk, knit to last 3 sts, k2tog, k1; N2: work as for N1—52 (60, 68) sts.

Rnd 2: Knit around.

Rep [Rnds 1 and 2] 9 times—16 (24, 32) sts rem with 8 (12, 16) sts on each needle.

FINISHING

Break yarn, leaving a 12" [31cm] tail. With tapestry needle and tail, graft toe closed using Kitchener st. Weave in ends. Block as desired.

STITCH AND COLOR KEY

☑ Sl 1 pwise

☐ Knit on RS, purl on WS

⊟ Purl on RS, knit on WS

⬚ K1-tbl on RS, p1-tbl on WS

Sl 2 to cn and hold in back, k2, k2 from cn

Sl 2 to cn and hold in front, k2, k2 from cn

■ On CC rnds, knit with CC
On MC rnds, slip with yarn to WS

■ On MC rnds, knit with MC
On CC rnds, slip with yarn to WS

Note: Each row of the color chart is worked twice. The colored boxes at the right of the chart indicate the color yarn used on each rnd.

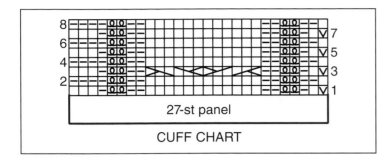

CUFF CHART

27-st panel

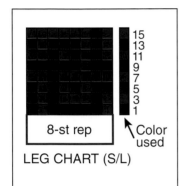

8-st rep

Color used

LEG CHART (S/L)

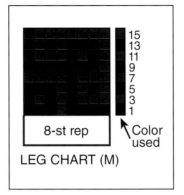

8-st rep

Color used

LEG CHART (M)

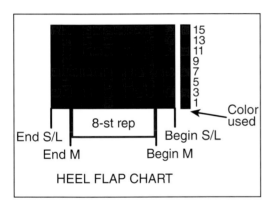

End S/L
End M
8-st rep
Begin S/L
Begin M

Color used

HEEL FLAP CHART

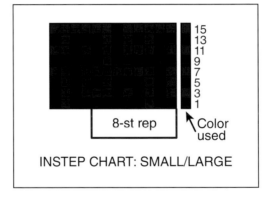

8-st rep

Color used

INSTEP CHART: SMALL/LARGE

BAVARIAN TWISTED STITCHES SOCKS

DESIGN BY JANEL LAIDMAN

Since the eighteenth century, knitters in the Austria/Bavaria region have been using twisted stitches to adorn their garments, evolving this art form into a highly patterned style rich with texture and ornament. These stitch patterns were passed down from one generation to the next through the use of swatches as stitch libraries. Today, knitters around the world have access to these patterns and enjoy making these visually pleasing works of art. ❧

Sizes
Woman's small [US size 5–6] (medium [US size 7–9], large [US size 9–12]). Instructions are given for smallest size, with larger sizes in parentheses. When only 1 number is given, it applies to all sizes.

Finished Measurements
Foot circumference: 7½ (8½, 9½)" [19 (21.5, 24)cm]

Materials 🧶**1**
♦ Lorna's Laces Shepherd Sock (fingering weight; 80% superwash wool/20% nylon; 215 yds [197m] per 2 oz [56g] skein): 1 skein Firefly

♦ Size 1 [2.25mm] double-pointed needles (set of 5) or size needed to obtain gauge

♦ Cable needle

♦ Tapestry needle

Gauge
32 sts and 44 rnds = 4" [10cm] in St st.

Adjust needle size as necessary to obtain correct gauge.

PATTERN NOTES

- This sock is made from the cuff down, with a flap heel, gussets, and a wedge toe.
- To change the size, change the stitch count by adding or removing purl stitches between the charts (revising stitch counts throughout pattern as necessary), or change the gauge by using a heavier/lighter weight yarn or larger/smaller needles.
- Crossed stitches are less elastic than other stitches. Try on your sock as you progress to make sure it is fitting and able to go over your heel. A snug fit in the ankle is normal.

STITCH PATTERNS

Rib (multiple of 4 sts)
Pattern rnd: *K2-tbl, p2; rep from * around.

BAVARIAN PATTERNS

See Charts A–E.

EYE OF PARTRIDGE

Row 1 (RS): *Sl 1, k1; rep from * across.
Row 2: *Sl 1, p1; rep from * across.
Rep Rows 1 and 2 for pat.

INSTRUCTIONS

CUFF

CO 64 (68, 72) sts. Distribute sts evenly across 4 dpns as follows: back of leg (N1 and N2): 32 (34, 36) sts and front of leg (N3 and N4): 32 (34, 36) sts. Mark beg of rnd and join, taking care not to twist your sts.

Work Rib pat for 6 rnds.

LEG

Set-up rnd: N1 and N2: work Chart C over 4 sts; Chart D over 6 sts, Chart E over 12 (14, 16) sts, Chart D over 6 sts, and Chart C over 4 sts; N3 and N4: work Chart A over 8 sts, Chart B over 16 (18, 20) sts, and Chart A over 8 sts.

Work even in est pats for 35 rnds—2 reps of charts are complete.

HEEL FLAP

Slip sts from N2 to N1 for heel; sts on other 2 dpns will remain on hold for instep.

Working back and forth on heel sts only, work Eye of Partridge pat for 30 rows.

TURN HEEL

Row 1 (RS): K18 (18, 20), ssk, k1; turn.

Row 2: Sl 1, p5 (3, 5), p2tog, p1; turn.

Row 3: Sl 1, knit to 1 st before gap formed on previous row, ssk (1 st on each side of gap), k1; turn.

Row 4: Sl 1, purl to 1 st before gap formed on previous row, p2tog (1 st on each side of gap), p1; turn.

Rep [Rows 3 and 4] 4 (5, 5) times—1 st rem each side of heel.

Next row: Sl 1, knit to 1 st before gap, ssk; turn.

Next row: Sl 1, purl to 1 st before gap, p2tog; turn—18 (18, 20) sts on needle.

GUSSET

Pick-up rnd: N1 (now heel/sole sts): Sl 1, knit across heel sts; with same dpn, pick up and knit 16 sts along side of heel flap; N2 and N3 (now instep sts): work Charts A, B, A as est; N4 (now heel/sole sts): pick up and knit 16 sts along other side of the heel flap, k9 (9, 10) sts from N1—82 (84, 88) sts with 50 (50, 52) heel/sole sts and 32 (34, 36) instep sts.

Rnd 1: N1: Knit to last 3 sts, k2tog, k1; N2 and N3: work Charts A, B, A as est; N4: k1, ssk, knit to end—80 (82, 86) sts.

Rnd 2: Work even.

Rep [Rnds 1 and 2] 8 (7, 7) times—64 (68, 72) sts with 32 (34, 36) sts each on instep and sole.

FOOT

Work even in est pats until foot measures approx 2" [5cm] short of desired length.

TOE

Rnd 1: Knit around.

Rnd 2: *N1: Knit to last 3 sts, k2tog, k1; N2: k1, ssk, knit to end; rep from * on N3 and N4—60 (64, 68) sts.

Rep [Rnds 1 and 2] 9 (11, 11) times—24 (20, 24) sts with 6 (5, 6) sts per dpn.

With N4, knit across sts on N1; slip sts from N3 to N4—12 (10, 12) sts on each dpn.

FINISHING

Cut yarn, leaving a 15" [38cm] tail. With tapestry needle and tail, graft toe closed using Kitchener st. Weave in ends. Block as desired.

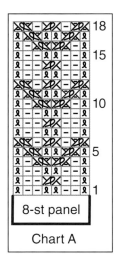

8-st panel

Chart A

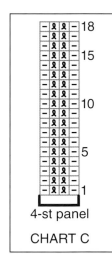

4-st panel

CHART C

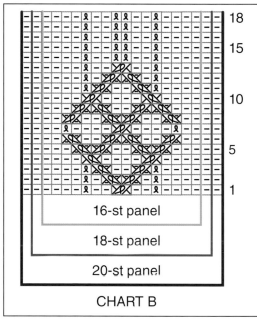

16-st panel

18-st panel

20-st panel

CHART B

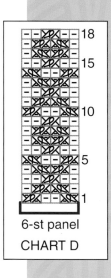

6-st panel

CHART D

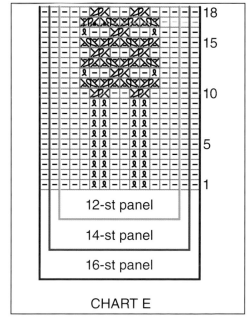

12-st panel

14-st panel

16-st panel

CHART E

STITCH KEY

☐ Knit

⊟ Purl

ℛ K1-tbl

⬚⬚ Sl 1 to cn and hold in back, k1-tbl, k1 from cn

⬚⬚ Sl 1 to cn and hold in front, k1, k1-tbl from cn

⬚⬚ Sl 1 to cn and hold in back, k1-tbl, p1 from cn

⬚⬚ Sl 1 to cn and hold in front, p1, k1-tbl from cn

☐ Panel for Small

☐ Panel for Medium

☐ Panel for Large

LITHUANIAN COLORWORK SOCKS

DESIGN BY DONNA DRUCHUNAS

In Lithuania, knitting was traditionally used only for small items such as mittens, gloves, and socks. Stitch patterns in geometric designs and with motifs inspired by nature, originally used in weaving, were adopted by knitters. Colorwork and handspun wool yarn were used to make warm winter socks such as these, which I've adapted for modern knitters. ❧

Sizes
Woman's medium (large, —) [US sizes 5-7 (8-12, —) / Man's small (medium, large) [US sizes 7–10 (10½–12, 12½–14)]

Instructions are given for smallest size, with larger sizes in parentheses. When only 1 number is given, it applies to all sizes.

Finished Measurements
Circumference: 7½ (9, 10½)" (19, [23, 26.5]cm)
Foot length: As desired to fit

Materials ②
◆ Brown Sheep Nature Spun Sport (sport weight; 100 percent wool; 184 yds [168m] per 1¾ oz [50g] ball): 2 balls Ash #720S (MC); 1 (1, 2) balls Nordic Blue #N30S (CC)

◆ Size 0 [2mm] double-pointed needles (set of 5)

◆ Size 2 [2.75mm] double-pointed needles (set of 5)

◆ Size 3 [3.25mm] double-pointed needles (set of 5) or size needed to obtain gauge

◆ Tapestry needle

Gauge
32 sts and 32 rnds = 4" [10cm] in stranded 2-color St st on larger dpns.

Adjust needle size as necessary to obtain gauge.

PATTERN NOTES

- This sock is worked from the cuff down with a "stair-step" heel flap, gusset, and spiral toe.
- The left and right socks are identical except that the arrows on Chart A face in opposite directions.
- Carry stranded yarn loosely to maintain elasticity of sock.
- If using suggested yarn, gently hand-wash the socks to prevent felting.

INSTRUCTIONS

CUFF

With MC and smallest dpn, CO 60 (72, 84) sts. Distribute evenly on 4 dpns, mark beg of rnd and join, taking care not to twist sts.

Work in K2, P2 rib for 6 rnds.

Change to CC and continue rib for 1½ (2, 2)" [3 (5, 5)cm].

Change to MC and work in ribbing for 6 rnds.

LEG

Change to largest dpns.

Rnds 1–6: Knit.

Rnds 7–23: Work Chart A for left or right sock.

Rnds 24–38: Work Chart B.

Rnds 39–44: Change to mid-size dpns; with MC, knit 6 rnds, or until leg is desired length.

Break MC.

STAIR-STEP HEEL FLAP

First step

Row 1 (RS): With 1 dpn and CC, knit across first 30 (36, 42) sts for heel; turn, leaving rem 30 (36, 42) sts on 2 dpns to hold for instep.

Row 2: Sl 1, k2, purl to last 3 sts, k3.

Row 3: Sl 1, knit to end.

Rep Rows 2 and 3 until the heel flap is half the desired length (approximately half of the width of the heel), ending with a WS row.

Second step

Count the number of slipped sts on one side of the flap.

Row 1 (RS): Knit the number of sts counted above (10 maximum), then put them on a holder or spare needle; knit across row until the same number of sts remains and put them on a holder or spare needle; turn.

Row 2: Sl 1, k2, purl to last 3 sts, k3.

Row 3: Sl 1, knit to end.

Rep Rows 2 and 3 until second step has same number of rows as first step, ending with a WS row. Break CC.

HEEL TURN AND PARTIAL GUSSET

Pick-up row (RS): With RS facing, join MC in the right-side corner of the 2 steps; using spare dpn, pick up and knit 1 st in each edge st up the side of the second step, then knit to center of heel; with another dpn, knit rem heel sts, then pick up and knit 1 st in each edge st down the other side of the heel center; slip the first st of the held side sts kwise, then pass the last picked-up st over it; turn.

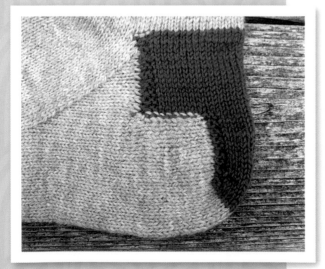

Row 2: Sl 1 purlwise, purl to the held sts on the other side; slip the first held st pwise and pass the last purled stitch over it; turn.

Row 3: Sl 1 knitwise, knit to the held sts; sl first held st kwise and pass the last knit st over it; turn.

Rep Rows 2 and 3 until all sts are worked, ending after working Row 2; turn.

GUSSET

Pick-up rnd: N4: Sl 1, knit to end (center heel); N1: knit to end, then pick up and knit 1 st in each edge st along the side of first step; N2 and N3: knit across the held instep sts; N4: pick up and knit 1 st in each edge st along the other side of the heel flap, then knit to end (center heel). Mark the new beg of rnd.

Rnd 2 (dec): N1: Knit to last 3 sts, k2tog, k1; N2 and N3: knit across; N4: k1, ssk, knit to end— 2 sts dec'd.

Rnd 3: Knit.

Rep [Rnds 2 and 3] until 60 (72, 84) sts rem.

FOOT

Work even until foot measures approx 2 (3, 3½)" [5 (7.5, 9)cm] short of desired finished length. Break MC.

SPIRAL TOE

Change to CC and knit around, dec 4 (0, 4) sts evenly around—56 (72, 80) sts.

Note: When working the toe, always knit the same number of rnds between dec rnds as you have knit sts between decs.

Spiral dec rnd 1: *K6 (7, 8), p2tog; rep from * around—49 (64, 72) sts.

Knit 6 (8, 7) rnds even.

Spiral dec rnd 2: *K5 (6, 7), p2tog; rep from * around—42 (56, 64) sts.

Knit 5 (6, 7) rnds even.

Spiral dec rnd 3: *K4 (5, 6), p2tog; rep from * around—35 (48, 56) sts.

Knit 4 (5, 6) rnds even.

Continue in this manner, decreasing 1 more st each dec rnd until you have worked last Spiral dec rnd as follows:

Last spiral dec rnd: *K1, p2tog; rep from * around—14 (16, 16) sts.

Last rnd: K2tog around—7 (8, 8) sts.

FINISHING

Break yarn, leaving a 6" [15cm] tail. Using tapestry needle, thread tail through rem sts, and pull tight. Weave in all ends. Wash and block if desired.

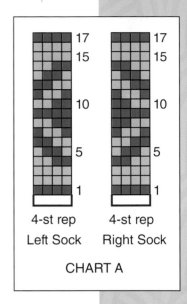

4-st rep
Left Sock

4-st rep
Right Sock

CHART A

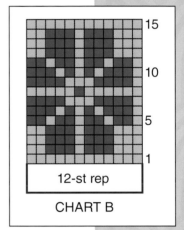

12-st rep

CHART B

COLOR KEY
☐ MC
■ CC

BOSNIAN SLIPPER SOCKS

DESIGN BY DONNA DRUCHUNAS

This fascinating Bosnian toe-up sock that has a rectangular toe that is knitted flat, but without purls! The rest of the sock is knitted in-the-round with an "after thought" short-row heel and crochet finishing. Inspired by slipper socks made in Bosnia-Herzegovina, the decorative embroidery adds an extra splash of color without the need to knit with more than two colors on any row. ❧

Sizes
Woman's medium [US size 6–9] (large [US size 8–11], extra large [US size 12])

Instructions are given for smallest size, with larger sizes in parentheses. When only 1 number is given, it applies to all sizes.

Finished Measurements
Foot circumference: 8 (8¾, 9½)" [20 (22.5, 24)cm]

Foot length: As desired.

Materials 2
- Reynold's *Soft Sea Wool* (sport weight; 100% wool; 162 yds [148m] per 1¾ oz [50g] ball): 1 ball each Red #0969 (MC) and White #0263 (CC)

- Approx 5 yds [5m] of 3 different colors of sport-weight yarn for embroidery
- Size 2 [2.75mm] double-pointed needles (set of 5)
- Size 4 [3.5mm] double-pointed needles (set of 5) or size needed to obtain gauge
- Spare circular needle or waste yarn
- Size E-4 [3.5mm] crochet hook
- Tapestry needle

Gauge
30 sts and 30 rnds = 4" [10cm] in stranded 2-color St st on larger dpns.

Adjust needle size as necessary to obtain correct gauge.

PATTERN NOTES

- These socks are worked from the toe up. The entire sock is worked in the round except for the initial portion of the toe. The heel is a peasant heel and is worked after the rest of the sock is complete. The ruffle edging on the cuff is crocheted.
- If using suggested yarn, gently hand-wash the socks to prevent felting.

SPECIAL ABBREVIATIONS

M1L (Make 1 Left): Insert LH needle from front to back under the running thread between the last st worked and next st on LH needle. With RH needle, knit into the back of this loop.

M1R (Make 1 Right): Insert LH needle from back to front under the horizontal loop between the last st worked and next st on LH needle. With RH needle, knit into the front of this loop.

INSTRUCTIONS

TOE

With MC, holding 2 smaller dpns tog and using long-tail method, CO 11 sts. Remove 1 dpn.

Row 1 (RS): K11, do not turn. Slide sts to other end of dpn and strand working yarn loosely across the back of your work so the sts lie flat and do not draw up into a tube

Rows 2-16: Rep Row 1; do not slide sts back after Row 16.

Pick-up rnd: With an empty dpn (N2), pick up and knit 13 sts along side edge of rectangle; with another dpn (N3), pick up and knit 10 sts along cast-on edge; with a 3rd empty dpn (N4), pick up and knit 14 sts along other side; mark beg of rnd—48 sts total.

Rnd 2: Knit around, rearranging sts so you have 12 sts on each of 4 dpns.

FOOT

Change to larger dpns and join CC.

With N1 and N2, work Chart A across 24 sole sts; with N3 and N4, work Chart B across 24 top-of-foot sts, increasing and maintaining MC at outer edges as indicated, then work charts even until foot measures desired length to beg of heel—60 (68, 72) sts.

PREPARE PEASANT HEEL OPENING

With waste yarn, work across the first 29 (33, 35) sole sts. Slip the last sole st onto the needle holding the instep sts. Start over again at beg of rnd and with MC, knit all the way around.

ANKLE

With MC, knit 4 rnds.

Work Chart C until ankle measures 2″ [5cm].

With MC, knit 4 rnds.

Do not bind off. Put sts on spare circular needle or waste yarn.

CROCHET RUFFLE EDGING

Rnd 1: With CC, sc in each live st around. Join with a slip st. (Remove waste yarn if you used it.)

Rnd 2: *Sc in next sc, ch3, sl st to first (bottom) ch, sc2tog; rep from * around. Join with a slip st and fasten off.

HEEL

Remove waste yarn and put heel sts onto 4 dpns; beg of rnd is at side between bottom of sole/heel and back of heel.

Join MC at beg of sole/heel sts.

Rnd 1: N1 and N2 (sole sts): Cont Chart B as est across 29 (33, 35) sts, M1L with MC; N3 and N4 (back heel): work Chart B pat as for sole across 29 (33, 35) sts, M1L with MC—60 (68, 72) sts.

Rnds 2–6: Maintaining edge sts in MC and diagonal stripe pat on sole and back of heel, work even following Chart B.

Dec rnd: N1: *With MC, ssk, work in pat to end; N2: work in pat to last 3 sts, k2tog with MC, k1; N3 and N4: rep from * across—56 (64, 68) sts.

Rep Dec rnd [every rnd] 12 (14, 15) times—8 sts.

BO knitwise with MC.

FINISHING

Turn sock inside out and whip st heel closed. Embellish with duplicate st embroidery as desired. Weave in ends. Wash and block if desired (see photos).

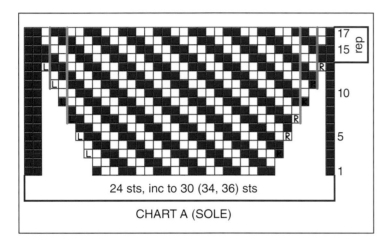

17
15
rep
10
5
1

24 sts, inc to 30 (34, 36) sts

CHART A (SOLE)

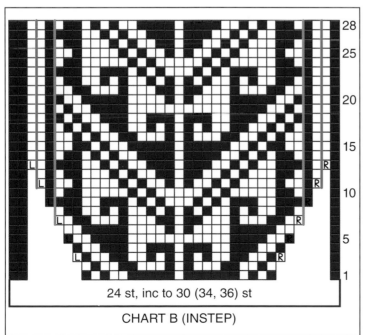

28
25
20
15
10
5
1

24 st, inc to 30 (34, 36) st

CHART B (INSTEP)

STITCH AND SIZE KEY

■ MC
□ CC
Ⓡ M1R with color indicated
Ⓛ M1L with color indicated
| Medium: Increase to here then work even.
| Large: Increase to here then work even.
Extra Large: Work entire Chart B.

4
1

4-st rep

CHART C

ALBANIAN ANKLETS

DESIGN BY DONNA DRUCHUNAS

When I visited the Bankfield Museum in Halifax England in 2008, I was amazed by the elaborate knitted items that Edith Durham collected in the Balkans in the early years of the twentieth century. These anklets are my version of the Albanian socks, made with a two section "swirl toe," which begins with a Turkish figure-eight cast on. In the Balkans, knitters make socks in the Eastern toe-up method that is also used in Turkey. Unique to Albanian socks, however, is the gathered heel that takes its shape from a section of rapid decreasing completed just before knitting the ankle and leg. These socks are made in heavier yarns, allowing the knitter to sample the techniques without investing so much time. ✎

Sizes
Woman's medium (large, —) [US sizes 6–9 (8–12, —)] / Man's small (medium, large) [US sizes 8½–10 (10½–12, 12½–14)]

Finished Measurements
Foot circumference: 8 (9, 10)" [20, (22.5, 25)cm]

Foot length: As desired to fit

Materials ④
◆ Mission Falls *1824 Wool* (worsted weight; 100% wool, 85 yds [78m] per 1¾ oz [50g] ball): 1 (2, 2) balls Charcoal #04 (MC), 1 (1, 2) balls Zinnia #26 (B), 1 ball each Natural #001 (C) and Dijon #014 (D)

◆ Size 4 [3.5mm] double-pointed needles (set of 5)

◆ Size 6 [4mm] double-pointed needles (set of 5) or size needed to obtain gauge

◆ Tapestry needle

Gauge
24 sts and 22 rnds = 4" [10cm] in stranded two-color stockinette stitch on larger dpns.

Adjust needle size as necessary to obtain correct gauge.

PATTERN NOTES

- Socks are worked from the toe up with a Turkish Figure-8 cast-on and a swirl toe (the toe swirls in opposite directions on left and right socks). The heel flap goes *beneath* the heel; the heel is turned when the sole is as long as the wearer's foot (toe to heel).
- Carry stranded yarn loosely to maintain elasticity of sock.
- If using suggested yarn, gently hand-wash the socks to prevent felting.

SPECIAL ABBREVIATIONS

M1L (Make 1 Left): Insert LH needle from front to back under the running thread between the last st worked and next st on LH. With RH needle, knit into the back of this loop.

M1R (Make 1 Right): Insert LH needle from back to front under the horizontal loop between the last st worked and next st on LH needle. With RH needle, knit into the front of this loop.

SPECIAL TECHNIQUE

Turkish Figure-8 Cast-On: Holding two double-pointed needles together with the yarn tail at the left, wrap the yarn around both needles, crossing between the needles in a figure-8 pattern, until the number of wraps equals half the number of stitches needed. Draw the yarn tightly around the needles. *Note: The loops on the lower dpn will be twisted, so you will work through the back loops of those sts on the first rnd.*

INSTRUCTIONS

TOE

With larger dpns and B, and using Turkish Figure-8 method, CO 14 (16, 18) sts.

Slide the bottom needle out a little toward the right, past the wraps, but do not remove it. With a 3rd needle, knit across the sts on the top needle. Cross the tail over the working yarn to secure it. Rotate the needles 180 degrees and knit through the backs of the unworked loops on the 2nd dpn—14 (16, 18) sts worked.

Rnd 1: *K7 (8, 9) sts on the first needle (N1), then with an empty needle (N2), pick up and knit 1 st on the side of the knitting; rep from * once working across the 3rd needle (N3), then picking up and knitting 1 st with a 4th needle (N4)—16 (18, 20) sts.

Rnd 2 (right sock only): *N1: knit; N2: knit to end, M1R; rep from * on N3 and N4—18 (20, 22) sts.

Rnd 2 (left sock only): *N1: knit; N2: M1L, knit to end; rep from * on N3 and N4—18 (20, 22) sts.

Rep [Rnd 2] 15 (18, 21) times—48 (56, 64) total sts with 7 (8, 9) sts on N1 and N3 and 17 (20, 23) sts on N2 and N4. The rest of the sock is worked the same for left and right.

Work 1 rnd even. Cut B.

FOOT

Redistribute sts so that there are 12 (14, 16) sts on each dpn.

Rnds 1–9: Work Chart A.

Work Chart B until foot is desired length to front of ankle/instep, ending with an odd-number row.

HEEL FLAP

Row 1 (RS): Work Chart B as est across first 24 (28, 32) sole sts; turn, leaving rem sts on hold for instep.

Cont working Chart B back and forth on 24 (28, 32) sole sts only until heel reaches just past the back of heel on foot, ending with Row 3 or 7 of chart. Cut B.

TURN HEEL

Row 1 (RS): With MC, k2tog across, turn—12 (14, 16) sts.

Row 2: P2tog across, turn—6 (7, 8) sts.

Beg working in rnds again as follows:

Rnd 1: N1: K2tog, k2 ([k2tog, k1]; [k4]), k2tog—4 (4, 6) heel sts rem; pick up and knit 14 (16, 17) sts along side of heel; N2 and N3: knit across 24 (28, 32) instep sts; N4: pick up and knit 14 (16, 17) sts along other side of heel, then knit first 2 (2, 3) heel sts from N1—56 (64, 72) sts.

Rnd 2: Change to smaller dpns; k2tog, knit to last 2 sts, k2tog—54 (62, 70) sts.

LEG

Rnds 1 and 2: *N1: Knit to last 2 sts, k2tog; N2: ssk, knit to end; rep from * on N3 and N4—46 (54, 62) sts.

Rnd 3: K2tog, knit to last 2 sts, k2tog—44 (52, 60) sts rem.

Knit 3 rnds even.

Work K2, P2 Rib for 6" [12.5cm].

FINISHING

BO loosely in rib. Weave in ends. Wash and block if desired.

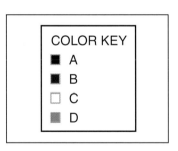

COLOR KEY
- ■ A
- ■ B
- □ C
- ▪ D

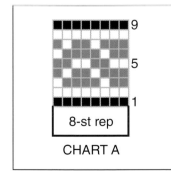

9

5

1

8-st rep

CHART A

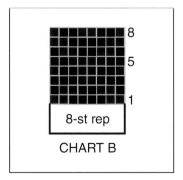

8

5

1

8-st rep

CHART B

SOCKS OF THE EAST

POPPY SOCKS: TURKISH SOCK

DESIGN BY ANNA ZILBOORG

This sock grows out of a traditional Turkish "hook" pattern (shown in the charts). It, in turn, developed from a motif used in rugs—as did most Turkish knitting patterns. The sock tradition in Turkey extends back toward the very beginning of knitting and continued into the twentieth century, when it quickly began to decline. Complexly patterned and many-colored socks were an integral part of village life in Turkey for hundreds of years. Turkish socks, most often used as indoor slippers, were knit for special celebrations and given as gifts for many occasions. This particular hook motif has appeared on wedding socks in horizontal bands of different colors, separated by bands of other patterns. Here the simple hooks change direction in the center front and center back of the sock. Each new repeat of the hook begins between the previous hooks on

Size
Woman's medium [US size 6–9]

Note: A larger sock can be made by using Socks that Rock medium weight (sport weight) and needles a size larger.

Finished Measurements
Length from top to ankle: 5" [12.5cm]

Foot circumference: 8" [20.5cm]

Materials 🧶1
◆ Blue Moon Fiber Arts Socks that Rock Lightweight (fingering weight; 100% superwash merino wool; 360 yds [329m] per 4½ oz [127g] skein): 1 skein each Strange Brew (MC) and Muckity Muck (CC)

◆ Size 2 [2.75mm] double-pointed needles (set of 5) or size needed to obtain gauge

◆ Size 3 [3.25mm] double-pointed needles (set of 5) or size needed to obtain gauge

◆ Stitch markers

Gauge
30 sts and 42 rows = 4" [10cm] in 1-color St st with smaller needles.

38 sts and 38 rows = 4" [10cm] in 2-color stranded St st with smaller needles.

32 sts and 35 rnds = 4" [10cm] in 2-color stranded St st with larger needles.

Adjust needle size as necessary to obtain correct gauge.

PATTERN NOTES

◆ This sock is worked from the toe up. It begins with a short-row toe, followed by a patterned instep that is worked back and forth. The solid-colored sole and gusset are also worked back and forth while being joined to the instep at each edge. The heel is turned with short rows, then the gusset stitches are joined to the heel flap with decreases. The leg is worked in the round and is fully patterned.

◆ When working the sole, add a second dpn when there are too many stitches for one dpn.

◆ The two socks are different from each other. The first sock uses one color for the sole and cuff and the second sock uses the other. The patterning also reverses MC and CC for the second sock.

SPECIAL ABBREVIATION

W&T (Wrap and turn): Slip next st from the LH needle. Bring the yarn to the RS between needles. Return the slipped st to LH needle. Turn the work around, bring yarn to WS, and continue in the other direction.

their last row. Both the figure and the ground are the same except where they change direction. I took this pattern from a book by Betsy Harrell called *Anatolian Knitting Designs* (Redhouse Press, 1981). It documents sock patterns from a knitting cooperative in Istanbul and provides information on the history and sociology of Turkish knitting. In that book, the pattern is knit in stripes of red and gold hooks on a black ground, which makes the pattern appear somewhat simpler than when it is worked in just two yarns. It is still surprising that something so conceptually simple becomes so visually complex and challenging to knit. ᵔ᲌

INSTRUCTIONS

TOE

With smaller dpns and MC, using long-tail method, CO 31 sts.

Work decreasing short rows as follows:

Row 1 (WS): Sl 1, p28, W&T.

Row 2: K27, W&T.

Row 3: P26, W&T.

Row 4: K25, W&T.

Continue in this manner, working one fewer stitch before W&T on each succeeding row, until you have worked k9, W&T.

Work increasing short rows while working Toe Chart as follows:

Row 1 (WS): P10, W&T.

Row 2: K11, W&T.

Row 3: P12, W&T.

Row 4: K13, W&T.

Row 5: Join CC and beg patterning; p14, W&T.

Continue working 1 more st each row until all 31 sts are in work.

INSTEP

Row 1 (RS): Sl 1 with MC (background color), cont Instep Chart to last st, k1 with MC.

Cont working 40-row chart, slipping first st and working last st with MC on each row, repeating pat as necessary until instep measures 2" [5cm] short of the desired length of the foot, ending with a purl row. *(Note last instep pat row worked; leg pat will begin with following row.)* Cut yarns.

Place a marker in the 15th slipped st from the last row on each side of the instep.

SOLE

Using smaller needles, pick up (but do not knit) 31 sts along the toe cast-on, including 1 st from each side of the instep to get the full number.

Row 1 (WS): Join MC; sl 1, purl to last st, slip last st pwise; with RH needle, pick up next st on instep pwise; insert LH needle into back of 2 sts on RH needle and p2tog; turn.

Row 2: Sl 1, knit to last st, slip last st kwise; with RH needle, pick up next slipped st on instep kwise, insert LH needle into front of 2 sts on RH needle and k2tog; turn.

Continue in this manner until you reach the markers.

GUSSET

Begin adding gusset sts.

Row 1 (WS): Sl 1, purl to end of row; pick up and purl under both legs of the slipped st on instep; turn— 32 sts.

Row 2: Sl 1, knit to end of row; pick up and knit under both legs of the slipped st on instep; turn—33 sts.

Rep [Rows 1 and 2] until all the slipped sts have been picked up—61 sole sts.

TURN HEEL

Place markers 14 sts in from each end of sole. The heel will be turned on the central 33 sts.

Set-up row (WS): Sl 1, p13, sm, p31; W&T.

Row 1: K29; W&T.

Row 2: P28; W&T.

Continue in this manner, working 1 st fewer before working W&T on each succeeding row until you have worked k9, W&T.

Next row (WS): P9, *pick up next wrap and lay it over the st it wrapped, purl the st and wrap tog; rep from * to the last wrapped st; pick up last wrap as before and purl it tog with its st and the next st; turn.

Next row: Sl 1, knit across picking up the wraps and knitting them together with their sts; at the last wrapped st, pick up the wrap and knit it together with its st and the next st; turn—31 heel sts.

HEEL FLAP/JOIN GUSSET

Row 1: Sl 1, purl to 1 st before gap left by turning on the last row, p2tog; turn.

Row 2: Sl 1, knit to 1 st before gap left by turning on the last row, ssk; turn.

Rep [Rows 1 and 2] until all 14 sts on the sides of the sole piece have been decreased—31 sts on needle. Cut yarn.

LEG

Mark center st of heel.

Shift the sts on the needles so that rnd begins 1 st after marked center heel and ends at the marked center heel st. Mark beg of rnd.

Work the Leg Chart around, beg with the pat row following the last row worked on the instep.

Work even, repeating the 40-rnd pat as necessary, until sock measures 4½″ [11.5cm] from the end of the heel flap, or desired length of leg.

CUFF

Work K1-tbl, P1 Rib for 7 rnds.

BO very loosely, preferably with the tubular bind-off.

SECOND SOCK

Work as for first sock, but reversing the colors. Weave in all ends. Block as necessary.

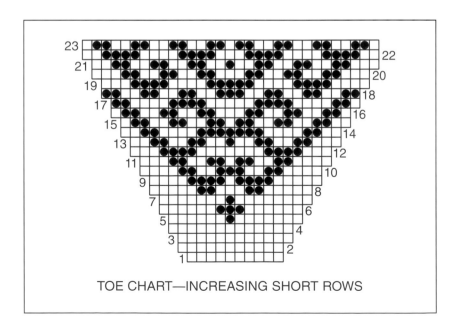

TOE CHART—INCREASING SHORT ROWS

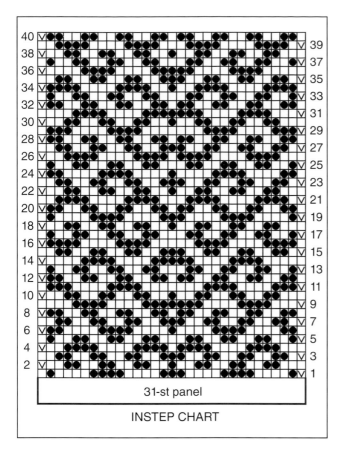

STITCH AND COLOR KEY
☐ With MC, k on RS, p on WS
● With CC, k on RS, p on WS
☑ Sl 1

Note: MC = sole color.
Sample socks reverse colors
for each sock.

31-st panel

INSTEP CHART

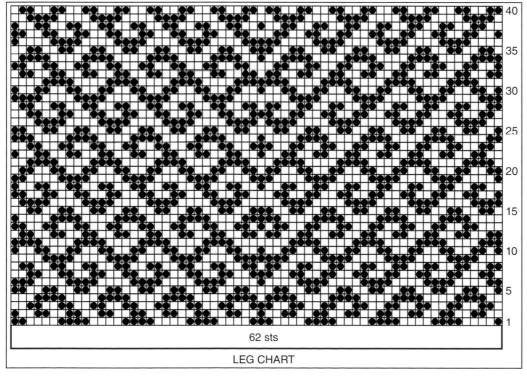

62 sts

LEG CHART

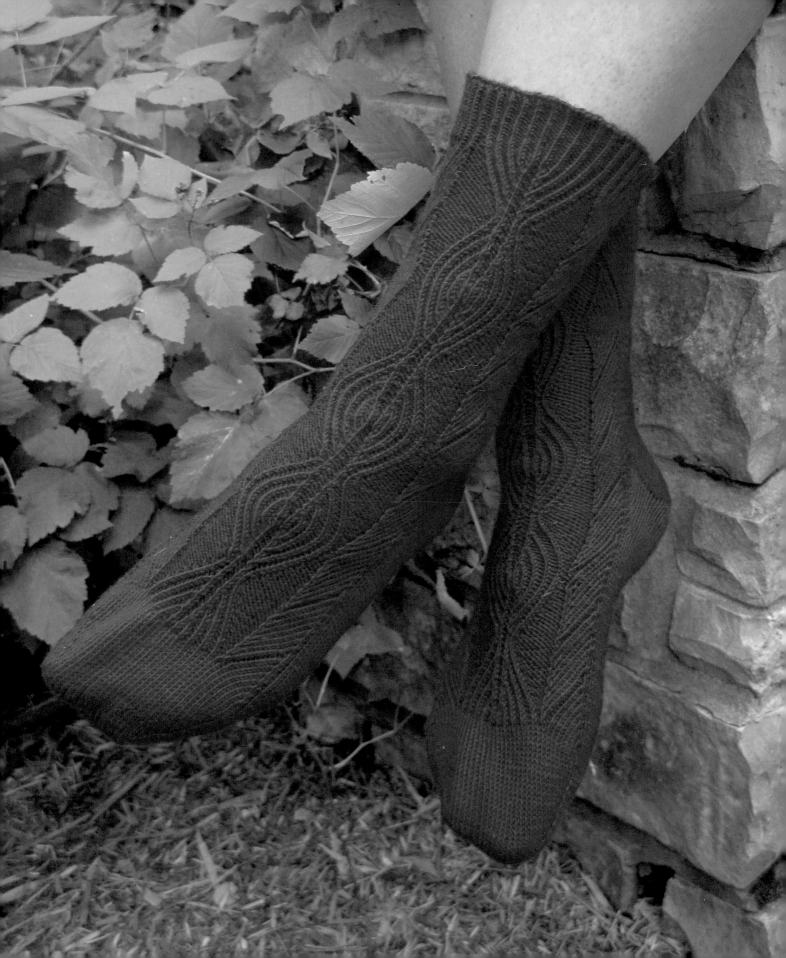

DURA-EUROPOS SOCKS

DESIGN BY ELANOR LYNN

My interest in the history of textile arts led me to cross the globe as well as two millennia to revive this elegant leaf and ogee textile design. My interpretation is derived from Barbara Walker's version in her 1970 masterpiece, *A Second Treasury of Knitting Patterns* (pages 139–140). She based her patterns on textile fragments excavated in the 1920s and 1930s from the Roman fort Dura-Europos (300 BC–256 AD) set high on the banks of the Euphrates River in present-day Syria. To quote Walker: "Knitter, let your hands reach back twenty centuries into the past and touch the hands of your unknown cultural ancestor who made that ancient fragment . . ."

At the time Walker published her patterns, the fragments were assumed to have been knitted. It is now generally believed that true knitting with two needles did not originate until at least 800–1000 CE and did not become widespread throughout the Middle East and Egypt until the Middle Ages. The original fragment was created

Sizes
Woman's small/medium [US sizes 6–8]

◆ *Sizing Options*: To create a proportionally larger sock, work on larger needles. For a longer foot, work more plain rounds after the toe before beginning the stitch patterns on the foot. For a sock with a greater circumference, add 1 or 2 purl stitches between the Ogee and Leaf patterns.

Finished Measurements
Foot circumference: 7½" [19cm]

Foot length: 9" [23cm]

Materials ❶
◆ Cascade *Heritage* (fingering weight; 75% wool/25% nylon; 437 yds [400m] per 3½ oz [100g] skein): 2 skeins red #5607

Note: You will need only a small amount of the second skein, if at all.

◆ Size 1 [2.25mm] double-pointed needles (set of 5)

◆ Size 2 [2.75mm] double-pointed needles (set of 5) or size needed to obtain gauge

◆ Size C/2 [2.75mm] crochet hook

◆ Stitch marker

◆ Tapestry needle

Gauge
40 sts and 50 rnds = 4" [10cm] in twisted St st (worked through the back loops) on larger needles.

Adjust needle size as necessary to obtain correct gauge.

PATTERN NOTES

- This sock is worked from the toe up, with an increasing wedge toe, an increasing gusset, a short-row heel turn, and a heel flap joined to gusset stitches.
- **Working through the back loops:** Every stitch, whether knitted or purled, is worked through the back loop (the few exceptions are noted in the pattern). To streamline the pattern, knit and purl stitches are assumed to be worked through the back loop, so if the pattern says "k1" or "p1," knit (or purl) the stitch through the back loop. Knitting through the back loop will create a severe amount of twist, especially on the sole.
- Practice the stitch patterns in tandem so you are confident with how the rounds match up before starting your project.

SPECIAL ABBREVIATIONS

Inc1 (lifted knit-knit inc): Insert tip of RH needle kwise into the head of the st below the next st on the LH needle; transfer this new loop the LH needle and knit it; knit next st.

P1K1inc (lifted purl-knit inc): Insert tip of RH needle kwise into the head of the st below the next st on the LH needle; transfer this new loop the LH needle and purl it; knit next st.

K1P1inc (lifted knit-purl inc): Insert tip of RH needle kwise into the head of the st below the next st on the LH needle; transfer this new loop the LH needle and knit it; purl next st.

W&T (Wrap and Turn): Bring yarn to RS of work between needles, slip next st pwise to RH needle, bring yarn around this st to WS, slip st back to LH needle, turn work to begin working back in the other direction. *Note: wraps will not be "joined" on later rows.*

SPECIAL TECHNIQUES

Provisional Cast-On: With crochet hook and waste yarn, make a chain several sts longer than desired cast-on. With knitting needle and project yarn, pick up indicated number of sts in the "bumps" on back of chain. When indicated in pattern, "unzip" the crochet chain to free live sts.

Decreases: The left-slanting decrease is worked k2tog-tbl. The right-slanting decrease is worked as k2tog, without working through the back loops.

by the earlier art of *naälbinding*, where fabric is formed by sewing freehand rows of interconnected loops. The results are remarkably similar to knitting. However, this older method is phenomenally tedious. I've managed to reproduce enough of this technique to understand how mind-numbing it can be to make a pair of socks in Dura-Europos patterns. These socks are a tribute the hyper-developed skills of our ancestors, which would make our clumsy modern hands wilt. For example, during the height of Renaissance knitting during the fifteenth and sixteenth centuries in Italy and France (for women in convents and for men in the guilds), most knitted articles were constructed at the unbelievably tiny gauge of 28–32 stitches to the inch. These socks, at 10 stitches to the inch, are quite coarse in comparison. ❧

STITCH PATTERNS

Leaf pattern (21-st panel, 16-rnd rep)

Ogee pattern (21-st panel; 32-rnd rep)

Inverted Leaf pattern (21-st panel; 16-rnd rep)

See charts.

INSTRUCTIONS

TOE

With smaller needles, using the provisional method, CO 21 sts.

Rows 1, 3 and 5 (RS): Knit, turn.

Rows 2, 4 and 6: Purl, turn.

Unzip the waste yarn from provisional cast-on and transfer 21 live sts to a 2nd dpn.

Pick-up rnd: N1: K11; N2: k10; pick up and knit 2 sts along side of rectangle; N3: pick up and knit 1 st along side of rectangle, k11 *(not tbl)*; N4: k10 *(not tbl)*, pick up and knit 2 sts along side rectangle, marking last st as beg of rnd; pick up and knit 1 more st and transfer to end of N1 (first st of next rnd)—48 sts, with 12 sts on each dpn.

Rnd 1: Chang to larger needles; sl 1 (transferred st), knit around, working all sts tbl.

Rnd 2 (inc): N1: *K2, Inc1, knit to end; N2: knit to last 3 sts, Inc1, k3; rep from * on N3 and N4—52 sts with 13 on each dpn.

Rnd 3: Knit.

Rep [Rnds 2 and 3] 8 more times—84 sts with 21 sts on each dpn.

Knit 8 rnds.

FOOT

Rnd 1 (set-up pats): N1: K1, k2tog-tbl, k6, P1K1inc (Leaf: left half); [p1, k1] 5 times, p1 (Ogee: right half); N2: [k1, p1] 5 times (Ogee, left half); K1P1inc, k6, k2tog, k2 (Leaf: right half); N3 and N4 (sole sts): k42.

Cont est pats through Rnd 48 (Leaf Rnd 16 and Ogee Rnd 16).

BEGIN GUSSET

Cont with est pats and inc 2 sts every other rnd to create gusset as follows:

Rnd 1 (inc): N1 and N2: (instep): Cont in est pat; N3 and N4: (sole sts): Inc1, knit to last st, Inc1.

Rnd 2: Work even.

Rep [Rnds 1 and 2] 7 more times, ending with Leaf pat Rnd 16 and Ogee pat Rnd 32—100 sts distributed as 21-21-29-29.

SHORT-ROW HEEL TURN

Short rows will be worked in twisted St st on center 32 sole sts; other sts rem on hold for gusset and instep.

Set-up row (RS): N1 and N2: Work pats as est; N3: knit across; N4: knit to last 13 sts, W&T.

Row 2 (WS): P32; W&T.

Decreasing short rows

Row 3: Knit to 1 st before wrap on previous row; W&T.

Row 4: Purl to 1 st before wrap on previous row; W&T.

Rows 5-16: Rep [Rows 3 and 4] 6 times, ending with p18, W&T.

Increasing short rows

Row 17: K18; W&T. *Note: There are now 2 wraps on the st.*

Row 18: P18; W&T. *Note: There are now 2 wraps on the st.*

Row 19: Knit to double-wrapped st, k1 (double-wrapped st); W&T.

Row 20: Purl to double-wrapped st, p1 (double-wrapped st); W&T.

Rows 21–32: Rep [Rows 19 and 20] 6 times, ending with p32, W&T.

WORK HEEL FLAP AND JOIN TO GUSSET STITCHES

Row 33 (RS): K32, k2tog-tbl (last wrapped st and next st), turn.

Row 34: P33, p2tog (last wrapped st and next st), turn.

Row 35: K1, [k1, sl 1] 16 times, k2tog-tbl, turn.

Row 36: Rep Row 34.

Rows 37–48: Rep [Rows 35 and 36] 7 times.

Row 49: K1, [k1, sl 1] 16 times, k2.

Row 50: P36.

Row 51: K2, [k1, sl 1] 16 times, k3.

Row 52: P38.

Row 53: K3, [k1, sl 1] 16 times, k4.

Row 54: P40

Row 55: K4, [k1, sl 1] 16 times, k5.

Row 56: N3: Work Rnd 1 of left half of Leaf pat over first 10 sts, work Rnd 1 of right half of Ogee pat over next 11 sts; N4: work Rnd 1 of left half of Ogee pat over first 10 sts; work right half of Leaf pat over last 11 sts. Do not turn.

LEG

Rnds 1–17: Cont est pats, with N1 and N3 working left half of Leaf pat and right half of Ogee pat and N2 and N4 working left half of Ogee pat and right half of Leaf pat, ending with Rnd 18 of Ogee pat and Rnd 2 of Leaf pat.

Next rnd (Ogee Rnd 19): Inc 4 sts around by omitting the p2tog decs and increasing as follows: P8, k1, Inc1, p1, Inc1, k1, p8—88 sts.

Cont in pat through Ogee Rnd 32, incorporating new sts into pat by purling 1 additional st at each edge of Ogee pat.

INVERTED LEAF

Right sock: Replace Leaf pat with Inverted Leaf pat over N2 and N3, working left and right halves as before; work Leaf pat as est on N1 and N4.

Left sock: Replace Leaf pat with Inverted Leaf pat over N1 and N4; work est Leaf pat on N2 and N3.

Continue in pattern through Ogee pat Rnd 30; Inverted Leaf pat will work charted Rnds 1–16, then 3–18.

Next rnd: Work Leaf pat without incs or decs as follows: K7, p1, k5, p1, k7; work other pats as est.

Next rnd: Complete est pats.

CUFF

Change to smaller dpns.

Rnd 1 (dec): Work in P1, K1 Rib and dec 4 sts evenly around, maintaining rib—84 sts.

Rnds 2-15: Cont in est rib.

Rnd 16: *P1, yo, k1; rep from * around—126 sts.

Knitting the yo tbl, BO in est pat.

FINISHING

Weave in all ends. Block to finished measurements.

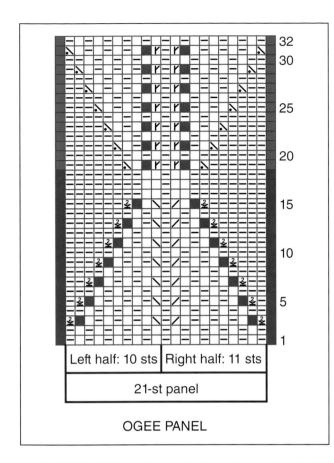

		32
		30
		25
		20
		15
		10
		5
		1

| Left half: 10 sts | Right half: 11 sts |
| 21-st panel |

OGEE PANEL

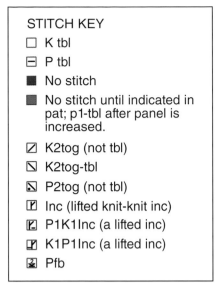

STITCH KEY

☐ K tbl

⊟ P tbl

■ No stitch

■ No stitch until indicated in pat; p1-tbl after panel is increased.

⧄ K2tog (not tbl)

⧅ K2tog-tbl

⧅ P2tog (not tbl)

Ⅳ Inc (lifted knit-knit inc)

Ⅳ P1K1Inc (a lifted inc)

Ⅳ K1P1Inc (a lifted inc)

₰ Pfb

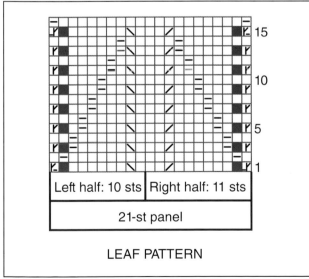

		15
		10
		5
		1

| Left half: 10 sts | Right half: 11 sts |
| 21-st panel |

LEAF PATTERN

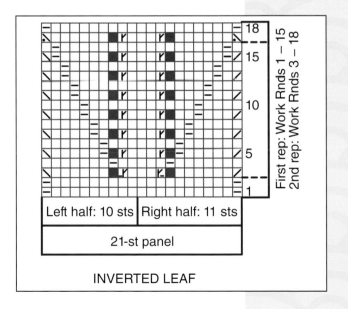

		18
		15
		10
		5
		1

First rep: Work Rnds 1 – 15
2nd rep: Work Rnds 3 – 18

| Left half: 10 sts | Right half: 11 sts |
| 21-st panel |

INVERTED LEAF

JAPANESE TABI SOCKS

DESIGN BY ANNIE MODESITT

Tabi are Japanese socks in which the big toe is separated from the other toes. Perfect for wearing with Geta sandals in Japan, or thongs in the West, they allow an agility that Western socks don't offer. Traditional Tabi, which have been worn in Japan since the 1500s, were sewn from cloth and had an open back with a row of buttons or clasps. These felted socks mimic the sturdy texture of the original fabric Tabi and include metal clasps up the back for closure. The socks are huge when knit, but will felt down to the size indicated in the finished measurement section. ❧

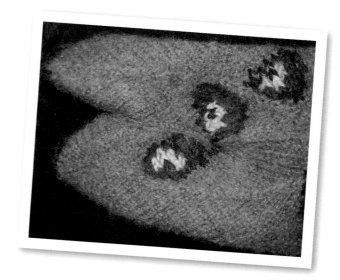

Sizes
Woman's small/medium [US size 3–7] (large/extra-large) [US size 7–12]. Instructions are given for smaller size, with larger size in parentheses. When only 1 number is given, it applies to both sizes.

Finished Measurements
Foot length (unfelted): 10 (12¼)" [25.5 (31)cm]

Foot length (felted): 8¾, 10¾" [22 (27.5)cm]

Slipper height (unfelted): 6½" [16.5cm]

Slipper Height (felted): 5¾" [14.5cm]

Materials 〔4〕
◆ Brown Sheep Yarn *Nature Spun* (worsted weight; 100% wool; 245 yds [224m] per 3½ oz [100g] ball): 1 ball each Red Fox #46 (A) and Impasse Yellow #305S (E); 2 balls Storm #114S (B); 1 (2) ball(s) each Tornado Teal #121 (C) and Limestone #144S (D)

◆ Size 7 [4.5mm] 24" [60cm] circular needle or size needed to obtain gauge

◆ Size 9 [5.5mm] 24" [60cm] circular needle or size needed to obtain gauge

◆ Locking stitch markers

◆ Tapestry needle

◆ 12 skirt hooks and eyes

◆ Sewing thread to match yarn

◆ Sewing needle

◆ Safety pins (optional)

Gauge
14 sts and 28 rows = 4" [10cm] in garter st with 2 strands of yarn held tog on larger needles (unfelted).

20 sts and 28 rows = 4" [10cm] in St st with 1 strand of yarn on smaller needles (unfelted).

Adjust needle size as necessary to obtain correct gauge.

PATTERN NOTES

◆ The sole of this slipper is worked in garter stitch with two strands of yarn held together with two toe sections at the end of the sole, one for the big toe and one for the four smaller toes. The top/upper of the slipper is worked in stockinette stitch with a single strand of yarn; it begins at the two toe sections and is gradually expanded to the back of the heel by picking up additional stitches along the sole; the back/heel end of the upper is shaped using short rows. The back of the slipper is split.

◆ Although the soles of the two toe sections have different stitch and row counts, the uppers for them are worked identically.

◆ The color motifs on the sides and top of the socks are worked partially with intarsia knitting and partially with duplicate stitch.

Gauge when felted:

20.5 sts and 32 rows = 4" [10cm] in garter st with 2 strands of yarn held tog on larger needles (felted).

22 sts and 32 rows = 4" [10cm] in St st with 1 strand of yarn on smaller needles (felted).

SPECIAL ABBREVIATIONS

S2KP2 (Centered Double Dec): Slip 2 sts as if to k2tog, k1, psso.

RIR (Raised Increase Right): Knit into st immediately below next st on needle, then knit next st.

RIL (Raised Increase Left): Knit next st, then knit into st 2 sts below st just worked.

W&T (Wrap and Turn): Slip next st to RH needle, wrap yarn around stitch and return to LH needle. Turn work and begin working back in the opposite direction. When working wrapped sts in row following short row, slip wrap up onto needle and work together with wrapped st.

SPECIAL TECHNIQUE

I-Cord Bind-Off: CO 3 sts; *k2, k2tog-tbl, do not turn. Sl 3 sts back to LH needle and rep from * across row until all sts are bound off. Bind off I-cord sts.

INSTRUCTIONS

SOLE (MAKE TWO)

With one strand each of A and B held tog and using larger needles, CO 7 (9) sts

Row 1 (inc): K2, kfb, knit to end—8 (10) sts.

Rep [Row 1] 9 (11) times—17 (21) sts.

Work even in garter st until there are 40 (48) rows/20 (24) garter ridges from beg.

Note: Mark both ends of last row with a piece of waste yarn.

Next row (inc): K2, kfb, knit to end—18 (22) sts.

Next row: Knit all sts

Rep last 2 rows 5 (7) times—23 (29) sts.

Work even in garter st until there are 12 (16) rows/6 (8) garter ridges following marked row. Remove markers.

BIG-TOE SECTION

Rows 1 and 3 (RS): K9 (11); turn, leaving rem 14 (18) sts unworked. Mark Row 1.

Row 2 and all WS rows: Knit.

Row 5 (dec): Ssk, knit to end—8 (10) sts.

Rep Row 5 [every RS row] 5 (7) times, ending with a WS row—3 sts.

Last row (RS): S2KP2. Fasten off last st.

FOUR-TOE SECTION

With RS facing, join one strand each A and B at point between the toe sections.

Row 1 and all RS rows: Knit all sts. Mark Row 1.

Row 2 (dec): Ssk, knit to end—13 (17) sts.

Rep Row 2 [every WS row] 7 (11) times, ending with a WS row—6 sts.

Next row: S2KP2 twice—2 sts.

Last row: K2tog; fasten off last st.

Weave in all ends on sole. Lay the soles down and turn one over so that they are positioned like left and right feet. Mark the left sole with one safety pin, the right sole with two; the pins are on the inside of the slipper sole.

FRONT UPPER

Row 1 (RS): With smaller needle and a single strand of D and "pin side" facing, beg at marked beg of toe and pick up and knit 9 (11) sts along the outer edge of toe section at right-hand side, 1 st at the tip (mark this st), 9 (11) sts along inside edge of same section, 1 st between toes (mark this st), 9 (11) sts up along inside edge of second toe section, 1 st at the tip (mark this st), and 9 (11) sts along outer edge—39 (47) sts.

Row 2 (WS): Purl to st between the toes, k1, purl to end.

Note: When picking up additional sts for front upper section, pick up 3 sts in every 4 rows/2 ridges, i.e., pick up new sts in both bumps and valleys along the sole edge.

Row 3: With a single strand of C, pick up and knit 1 st adjacent to D working yarn; knit to 1 st before marked tip st, S2KP2; knit to 1 st before marked st between toes, RIR, p1, RIL; knit to 1 st before marked tip st, S2KP2; knit to end, pick up and knit 1 st.

Row 4: With C, purl to st between the toes, k1, purl to end.

Rep [Rows 3 and 4] 12 (16) times more, alternating 2 rows D and 2 rows C, then work Row 3 once more with D—39 (47) sts. Cut C.

BACK UPPER

Right side

With RS facing and B, pick up and knit 19 (21) sts along the right edge of the sole and 7 (9) sts heel sts in cast-on edge.

First Short-Row Pair (WS & RS): P18 (20), W&T; knit back to beg of row.

Next Short Row Pair (WS & RS): Purl to 1 st before last wrapped st, W&T; knit back to beg of row.

Rep last short-row pair 5 more times—7 wrapped sts.

Next row (WS): With B, p26 (30), working sts and wraps tog as you come to them; change to D and work 39 (47) front sts as est; join B and pick up and purl 19 (21) sts along the left edge of the sole; using cable method, CO 7 (9) sts to form a flap—91 (107) sts.

Left side

First Short Row Pair (RS & WS): K18 (20), W&T; purl back to beg of row.

Next Short Row Pair (RS & WS): Knit to 1 st before last wrapped st, W&T; purl back to beg of row.

Rep last short-row pair 5 more times—7 wrapped sts.

COMPLETE UPPER AND LEG

Row 1 (RS): Beginning where indicated on Chart A, work intarsia as directed across 28 (30) sts, working sts and wraps tog as you come to them, place marker; cont working across front with C to last 28 (30) sts, working S2KP2s and purling center st as before, but discontinuing the raised incs; work Chart B across last 28 (30) sts—87 (103) sts.

Row 2 (WS): Working in colors as est and following charts at each end, purl to the center front st, k1, purl to end. *Be sure to strand D along work so it is in place for next RS row.*

Cont Charts A and B, working in est stripe pat across the center of the work between charts. Cont working S2KP2s each RS row 8 (10) times until no sts rem between S2KP2s and center purl st, then knit those sts on subsequent rows—55 (63) sts.

Cont until Charts A and B are complete.

With C, knit 4 rows.

With D, work I-cord bind-off across all sts.

Complete colorwork at sides following Duplicate Stitch Chart.

Using A, B, and E and duplicate st, add a few small free-form motifs in the stripe section (see photo).

FINISHING

Weave in ends.

Sew the center back flap *behind* the opposite center back edge for the Right sock (creating the Right back placket facing), and *in front* of the center back edge for the Left sock (creating the Left back placket)

Felt slippers to desired size in washing machine. While they are still wet, pull and stretch them into the desired shape. If necessary, steam the slippers to soften them up so they can be more easily formed to desired shape. Wearing them until they are dry will help them mold to your feet (pin the back closed).

Sew six skirt hooks to each back placket, sew the eyes to the facing to correspond to the hooks.

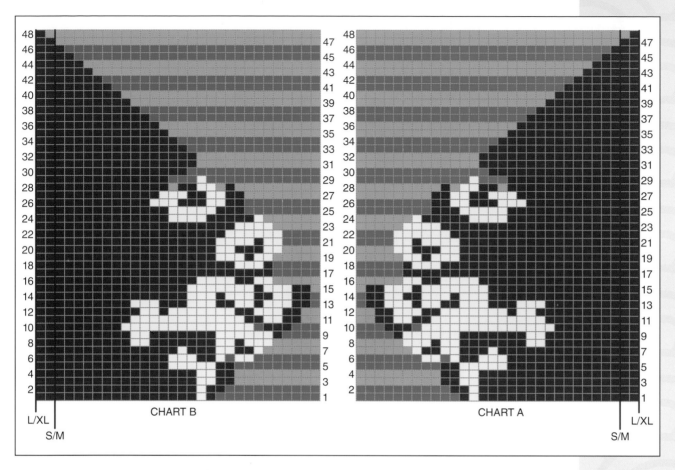

CHART B

CHART A

L/XL

S/M

L/XL

S/M

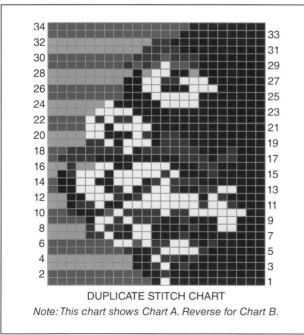

DUPLICATE STITCH CHART

Note: This chart shows Chart A. Reverse for Chart B.

COLOR KEY

- A
- B
- C
- D
- E

RUSSIAN-INSPIRED SOCKS

DESIGN BY TATYANA CHAMBERS

When I was growing up in Russia, my grandma would knit a pair of warm wool socks for me for each winter. They were never fancy, but always warm and sometimes fuzzy, if she had the right yarn. I learned how to knit socks when I was in fourth grade and knew how to turn heels without any written notes. Socks weren't a fancy accessory, but a necessity to keep your feet warm in the winter. They were always knit from wool and sometimes from goat's down, if one could afford it. Naturally, due to the choice of the yarn, they were fast knits. In this design, I decided to use sport-weight yarn and add a pattern.

Since knitting in Russia didn't became popular until the mid-seventeenth century, and even that was heavily influenced by other cultures, I've added traditional Russian embroidery motifs that were in use starting sometime before the tenth century as my inspiration. Embroidery motifs in Slavic culture were not just for making a garment pretty—each motif had a meaning and could provide its owner with protection from the evil eye, bring luck, increase fertility, and so on. Diamond-shaped motifs with "hooks" and solar symbols were especially popular in women's clothing;

Size
Woman's medium [US size 6–9]

FINISHED MEASUREMENTS
Circumference: 8" [20.5cm]

Foot length: Custom

Materials 2
◆ KnitPicks *Telemark* (sport weight; 100% Peruvian Highland wool; 103 yds [94m] per 1¾ oz [50g] skein): 2 skeins Poppy (MC), one skein Drift (CC)

◆ Size 3 [3.25mm] double-pointed needles (set of 5) or size needed to obtain gauge

◆ Stitch markers

◆ Stitch holder

◆ Tapestry needle

Gauge
24 sts and 30 rnds = 4" [10cm] in stranded 2-color St st.

Adjust needle size as necessary to obtain correct gauge.

PATTERN NOTES

◆ This sock is worked from the top down with a separate patterned instep section. The heel flap, heel turn, and gusset are all worked back and forth on the heel stitches. After the gusset is complete, the instep stitches are rejoined to the sole stitches and the foot is worked in the round to the toe. The instep is sewn to the gusset after the sock is complete.

◆ Strand the yarn not in use loosely on WS to maintain elasticity of fabric; do not carry yarn not in use more than 5 sts—weave it in as necessary.

SPECIAL ABBREVIATIONS

N1, N2, N3 N4: Needle 1, needle 2, needle 3, needle 4; after gusset is complete, N1 and N2 hold sole sts and N3 and N4 hold instep sts.

they had names like "frog" or "kolenki," and were believed to be symbols of fertility. They were also used above the entrance into a house for protection, or as a pattern on locks.

Traditionally, the background color is white with red motifs on it, but since we are talking about socks here, white might be not very practical, so I reversed the colors, making red the background. Red and white in Slavic culture are traditional colors and represent male and female energies, like the concepts of yin and yang in Asia. Feel free to use a traditional white background if you wish.

The purl round around the ankle of the sock below the ribbing is called *obruchok* and is believed to have be a charm that protects the wearer. ❧

STITCH PATTERNS

Obruchok (even number of sts)

Pattern rnd: Carrying both yarns in front of work with MC below CC, p1 MC, p1 CC.

Note: Do not twist the two strands of yarn as for a braid; always carry MC below CC.

INSTRUCTIONS

CUFF

With MC, CO 48 sts. Distribute sts evenly onto 4 dpns; mark beg of rnd and join, taking care not to twist sts.

Work K2, P2 Rib for 3" [7.5cm].

Next rnd: Work Obruchok pat.

LEG

Knit 6 rnds with MC.

Work 7 rnds following Chart A.

Knit 5 rnds with MC.

Next rnd: Knit across N1, N2 and N3; slip sts on N4 to N1 to hold for heel; slip sts on N3 to N2 for instep, turn work.

INSTEP

Worked back and forth on 24 sts on N2

Row 1 (WS): Purl.

Row 2 (set up pat): Work Chart B as follows: K4 MC, pm, join CC and work 15-st motif, pm, k5 MC.

Rows 3–11: Complete Chart B. Cut CC.

With MC, work 4 rows St st. Cut yarn, leaving a 4" [10cm] tail.

Instep sts will remain on hold until gusset is complete.

HEEL FLAP

With WS facing, join MC to N1.

Beg with a purl row, work 11 rows in St st.

HEEL TURN

Row 1 (RS): K17, ssk, turn.

Row 2: Sl 1, p10, p2tog, turn.

Row 3: Sl 1, k10, ssk, turn.

Row 4: Sl 1, p10, p2tog, turn.

Rep [Rows 3 and 4] 4 times, do not turn—12 sts rem.

GUSSET

Row 1: With WS still facing, pick up and purl 10 sts along edge of heel flap, turn—22 sts.

Row 2 (RS): K16 sts onto 1 dpn (now N1); with another dpn (now N2), k6, then pick up and knit 10 sts along other side of heel flap, turn—32 sts with 16 each on N1 and N2.

Row 3: Purl all sts.

Row 4: K1, ssk, knit to last 3 sts, k2tog, k1—30 sts.

Row 5: K1, purl to last st, k1.

Rep [Rows 4 and 5] 3 times—24 sts rem, with 12 sts on N1 and N2.

FOOT

Rnd 1: Knit across 24 sole sts on N1 and N2; knit across 24 instep sts now on N3 and N4; mark new beg of rnd—48 sts with 12 sts on each dpn.

Continue knitting until foot measures approx 2–2½" [5–6.5cm] short of desired total length.

TOE

Rnd 1 (dec): N1: K1, ssk, knit to end; N2: knit to last 3 sts, k2tog, k1; N3 and N4: work as for N1 and N2—44 sts.

Rnds 2 and 3: Knit around (if you have short feet, knit 1 rnd between dec rnds).

Rep Rnds 1–3—40 sts.

Rep [Rnds 1 and 2] 6 times—16 sts.

Transfer sts on N2 to N1 and sts on N4 to N3—8 sts on 2 dpns.

Cut yarn, leaving a 12" [30.5cm] tail.

With tapestry needle and tail, graft toe closed using Kitchener st.

FINISHING

Weave in all ends. Invisibly sew instep edges to gusset edges. Block socks, being careful not to flatten the rib.

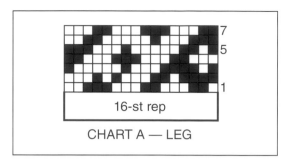

16-st rep

CHART A — LEG

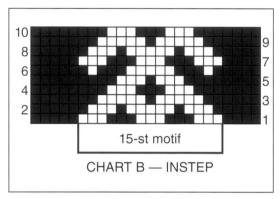

15-st motif

CHART B — INSTEP

CHINESE ZODIAC SOCKS

DESIGN BY PINPILAN WANGSAI

These socks were based on the sewn *tabi* socks made of cute fabrics and worn with a pair of wooden *getas*. Being a knitter, I immediately thought, "Hmm . . . I can knit these." The result is a slightly modern twist on the *tabi* sock. Knitting eliminates the seams on the bottom of the feet and makes for a better fit. I added a mock seam down the back of the foot like the ones a sewn pair would have so you can add a row of buttons for that extra cuteness factor. The heels and toes are done in contrasting color so the eyes are drawn to the unusual toes. I also added an intarsia design on the ankles for a bit of spice. You have your choice of twelve charted motifs based on the *kanji* of the Chinese zodiac signs—the motif on the pictured socks represents the Year of the Pig. These socks are worked from the toe up, so the tricky part is out of the way and you are left with only the fun bits. Enjoy! ❧

Sizes
Woman's medium [US size 6–9] (large) [US size 8–11]. Instructions are given for smaller size, with larger size in parentheses. When only 1 number is given, it applies to both sizes.

Finished Measurements
Foot circumference: 8 (8¾)" [20.5 (22)cm]

Length: Custom

Materials 🧶**1**
◆ Kanebo *Caprice* (fingering weight; 50% wool/ 50% acrylic; 226 yd [207m] per 1¾ oz [50g] skein): 1 skein each # 219 (MC) and #201 (CC)

◆ Size 2 [2.45mm] double-point needles (set of 4) or size needed to obtain gauge

◆ Size D/3 [3.25mm] crochet hook for provisional cast-on

◆ Stitch holders

◆ Stitch marker

◆ 6 buttons

Gauge
30 sts and 40 rnds = 4" [10cm] in St st.

Adjust needle size as necessary to obtain correct gauge.

PATTERN NOTES

- These socks are worked from the toe up with two sections for the toes: the first is for the outer four toes and the second for the big toe. After the foot is complete, a short-row heel is worked, followed by the leg, which is split for a back button placket and is knit with the motif worked on the outside half of the sock.

- The pattern on the leg is worked with the intarsia method (using separate lengths of yarn for each color area) rather than stranding. You have your choice of twelve charted motifs based on the kanji of the Chinese zodiac signs (the motif on the sample stands for the Year of the Pig).

SPECIAL ABBREVIATIONS

N1, N2, N3: Needle 1, needle 2, needle 3

W&T (Wrap and Turn): Bring yarn to RS of work between needles, slip next st pwise to RH needle, bring yarn around this st to WS, slip st back to LH needle, and turn work to begin working back in the other direction.

SPECIAL TECHNIQUES

Provisional Cast-On: With crochet hook and waste yarn, make a chain several sts longer than desired cast on. With knitting needle and project yarn, pick up indicated number of sts in the "bumps" on back of chain. When indicated in pat, "unzip" the crochet chain and place live sts on needle.

3-Needle Bind-Off: With RS tog and needles parallel, using a third needle, knit tog a st from the front needle with 1 from the back. *Knit tog a st from the front and back needles, and slip the first st over the second to bind off. Rep from * across, then fasten off last st.

Hiding wraps: On RS rows: pick up wrap(s) from front to back and knit tog with wrapped st. On WS rows, pick up wrap(s) from the back, then purl tog with wrapped st.

INSTRUCTIONS

FOUR-TOE SECTION

With CC and using provisional method, CO 11 (13) sts.

Beg with a RS row, work 4 rows in St st.

Unzip the waste yarn from the provisional CO and put the live sts on another dpn.

Rnd 1: N1: K11 (13) across first dpn; pick up and knit 1 st from side edge; N2: pick up and knit 1 st from side edge, k5 (6) sts from dpn holding CO sts; N3: k6 (7) rem CO sts, pick up and knit 2 sts from side edge; transfer last picked-up st to end of N1, mark beg of rnd—26 (30) sts with 13 (15) sts on N1, 6 (7) sts on N2, and 7 (8) sts on N3.

Rnd 2 and all even-numbered rnds: Knit around.

Rnds 3 and 5: N1: Kfb, knit to last st, kfb; N2: kfb, knit to end; N3: knit to last st, kfb—34 (38) sts.

Rnds 7, 9, 11, 13, 15: N1: Kfb, knit to end; N2: knit across; N3: knit to last st, kfb—44 (48) sts.

Rnds 16 and 17: Knit around.

Try on four-toe section; continue in St st until section is long enough to cover toes.

Slip first 18 (20) sts to a st holder; transfer next 8 st to waste yarn; slip last 18 (20) sts another st holder. Remove marker, break yarn, and set aside.

BIG-TOE SECTION

Using CC and provisional method, CO 5 (6) sts.

Beg with a RS row, work 4 rows in St st.

Unzip the waste yarn from the provisional CO and put the live sts on another dpn.

Rnd 1: N1: K5 (6) across first dpn; pick up and knit 1 st from side edge; N2: pick up and knit 1 st from side edge, k2 (3) sts from dpn holding CO sts; N3: k3 rem CO sts, pick up and knit 2 sts from side edge; transfer last picked-up st to end of N1, mark beg of rnd—14 (16) sts with 7 (8) sts on N1, 3 (4) sts on N2, and 4 sts on N3.

Rnd 2 and all even-numbered rnds: Knit around.

Rnds 3 and 5: N1: Kfb, knit to last st, kfb; N2: kfb, knit to end; N3: knit to last st, kfb—22 (24) sts.

Rnds 7, 9, 11: N1: Kfb, knit to end; N2: knit across; N3: knit to last st, kfb—28 (30) sts.

Rnds 12-17: Knit around.

Try on big-toe section; continue in St st until section is long enough to cover toe to base.

JOIN TOE SECTIONS

Transfer 8 sts of four-toe section from waste yarn to spare dpn.

First joining rnd: K10 (11) sts from big-toe section; join the 2 toe sections working 3-needle BO across next 8 sts and 8 sts on spare dpn; k10 (11) rem big-toe sts.

Note: The second Joining Rnd sets up the left and right foot; the needle arrangement is different for each sock.

Second joining rnd (right sock): K10 (11) sts of big-toe section; pick up and knit 2 sts from edge of join; k18 (20) sts from 4-toe holder (this will be N2); with another dpn, knit first 15 (17) sts from other st holder (this will be N3); with another dpn, k3 rem sts from holder, pick up and knit 2 sts from edge of join, k10 (11) rem sts of big-toe section (this will be N1)—60 (66) sts with 30 (33) sts on N2, 15 (17) sts on N3, and 15 (16) sts on N1.

Second joining rnd (left sock): K10 (11) sts of big-toe section; pick up and knit 2 sts from edge of join, knit first 3 sts from four-toe st holder (this will be N3); with another dpn, k15 (17) rem sts from st holder (this will be N1); k18 (20) sts from other st holder; pick up and knit 2 sts from edge of join; k10 (11) rem sts from big-toe section (this will be N2)—60 (66) sts with 15 (16) sts on N3, 15 (17) sts on N1, and 30 (33) sts on N2.

BOTH SOCKS

Break CC and rejoin at beg of N1; mark new beg of rnd.

Knit 5 rnds with CC. Break CC.

With MC, knit all rnds until foot measures approx 2" [5cm] short of your back heel.

SHORT-ROW HEEL

Set-up rnd: Knit to the end of N2, then change to CC, but don't break MC; with 1 dpn, knit across all sts on N3 and N1, turn—30 (33) heel sts. Sts on N2 rem on hold for instep while short-row heel is worked.

Short-row 1 (WS): Purl to last st on heel needle, W&T.

Short-row 2: Knit to last st on heel needle, W&T.

Short-row 3: Purl to st before wrapped st, W&T.

Short-row 4: Knit to st before wrapped st, W&T.

Rows Rep [Rows 3 and 4] 6 times—14 (17) stitches in the middle with 8 wrapped sts on either side.

Short-row 17 (WS): Purl to first wrapped st, hide wrap, W&T (st is double wrapped).

Short-row 18: Knit to first wrapped st, hide wrap, W&T (st is double wrapped).

Short-row 19: Purl to first double-wrapped st, hide wraps, W&T.

Short-row 20: Knit to first double-wrapped st, hide wraps, W&T.

Rep Rows 19 and 20 until all sts are live again.

Purl 1 row. Break CC.

LEG

Divide the heel sts with 15 (16) sts on N1 and 15 (17) sts on N3 as they were before working heel.

With MC (currently at end of N2) and free needle, pick up and knit 2 sts in gap between N2 and N3, then k15 (17) sts from N3; N1: K15 (16), then pick up and knit 2 sts in gap between N1 and N2; N2: k30 (33); N3: k17 (19); mark beg of rnd—64 (70) sts.

Rnds 2 and 4 (dec): N1: Knit to last 2 sts, k2tog; N2: knit; N3: ssk, knit to end—62 (68) sts.

Rnd 3: Knit.

Rnds 5-10: Knit.

Note: If you want the leg of your sock to be longer than the one shown in the picture, knit extra rnds here.

Split back leg and intarsia motif

Row 1 (right sock): N1: Knit; N2 and N3: k18 (22), pm, work Row 1 of chart showing desired motif across next 21 sts, pm; knit to end of N3, then pick up and knit 1 st in front of each of the first 3 sts on N1 to form overlapping back placket; turn to work a WS row—63 (69) sts.

Row 1 (left sock): N1 and 2: K6 (7), pm, work Row 1 of chart showing desired motif across next 21 sts, pm, knit to end of N2; N3: knit to end, then pick up and knit 1 st in front of each of the first 2 sts on N1 to form overlapping back placket; turn to work a WS row—63 (69) sts.

Row 2 (both socks): K6, purl to last 3 sts (working chart between markers), k3, then pick up and knit 1 st in each of the purl bumps below first 3 sts on N3 to form underlapping back placket, turn—66 (72) sts.

Maintaining 6-st garter plackets at both ends of back leg and intarsia pat between markers, work even until chart is complete. Break CC.

Knit 6 rows with MC.

Work 8 rows in K2, P2 rib.

BO very loosely in rib.

FINISHING

With plackets overlapped, sew back seam along inner placket edge. Sew on buttons, going through both placket layers. Weave in ends and get out your *getas*!

COLOR KEY
■ MC
□ CC

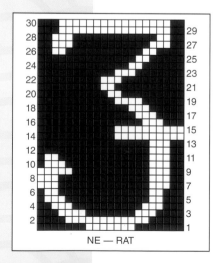

NE — RAT

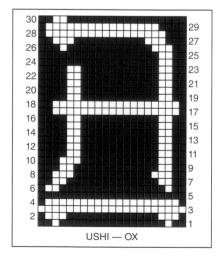

USHI — OX

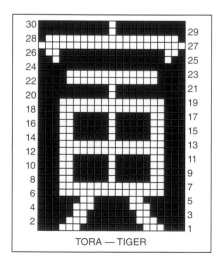

TORA — TIGER

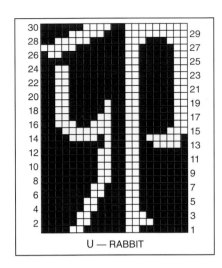

U — RABBIT

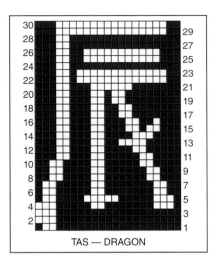

TAS — DRAGON

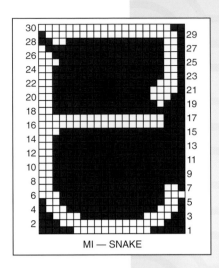

MI — SNAKE

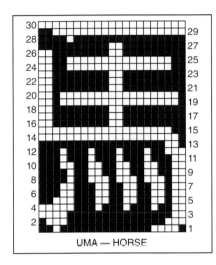

UMA — HORSE

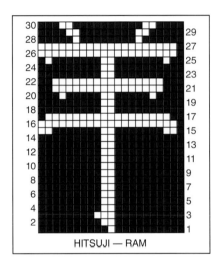

HITSUJI — RAM

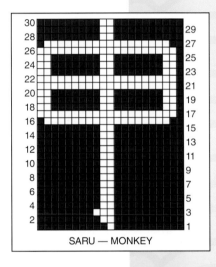

SARU — MONKEY

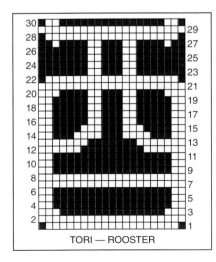

TORI — ROOSTER

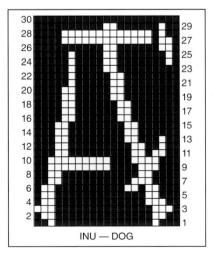

INU — DOG

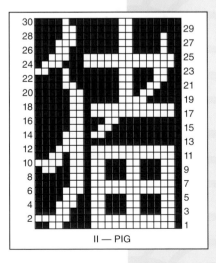

II — PIG

SOCKS OF THE WEST

MOSAIC BLUE JEANS SOCKS

DESIGN BY CANDACE EISNER STRICK

These fun socks employ the age-old technique of slip stitch knitting, made popular in the 1960s when American knitting icon Barbara Walker embraced the technique, calling it "Mosaic Knitting". Mosaic knitting allows the knitter to create a two-color pattern while handling only one yarn at a time. For best results, use two highly contrasting colors or a light and a dark color for A and B. Walker designed hundreds of new mosaic patterns, which can be found in *Mosaic Knitting* and her *Treasury of Knitting Patterns* books. ❧

Sizes

Woman's medium [US size 6–9] (large [US size 8–12])

Instructions are given for smaller size, with larger sizes in parentheses. When only 1 number is given, it applies to both sizes.

Finished Measurements

Top leg circumference: 8 (9)" [20 (23)cm]

Foot circumference: 8 (9)" [20.5 (23)cm]

Materials ①

◆ Lorna's Laces *Shepherd Sock* (fingering weight; 80% superwash wool/20% nylon; 435 yds [398m] per 3½ oz [100g] skein: 1 skein each Clara's Garden (A) and Blackberry (B) (*See Pattern Notes*)

◆ Size 1 [2.25mm] double-pointed needles (set of 4) or size needed to obtain gauge

◆ Size C-2 [2.75mm] crochet hook for provisional cast-on

◆ Tapestry needle

Gauge

32 sts and 40 rnds = 4" [10cm] in St st.

28 sts and 64 rows = 4" [10cm] in garter Mosaic pat.

36 sts and 40 rnds = 4" [10cm] in two-color stripe pat.

Adjust needle size as necessary to obtain correct gauge.

PATTERN NOTES

◆ The cuff and leg of this sock is worked back and forth in the garter-stitch mosaic pattern. After the leg is joined into a tube using the 3-Needle Bind-Off, stitches are picked up along the lower edge for the heel flap and instep, at which point the sock is worked in the round to the toe.

◆ The 2-Color Stripe pattern alternates A and B in Rnd 1, then B and A in Rnd 3. Because the gusset decreases will interrupt the color alternation between needles on some rounds, treat each needle as a separate "pattern", maintaining the A-B, then B-A alternations on Rnds 1 and 3. *Hint*: When working with N3 during the gusset shaping, the first few stitches of the alternating color pattern may have been interrupted by previous gusset decreases; look at the stitches of the previous 2-color rnd at least 4 sts in from the beginning of the needle to verify your stitch pattern. Once the gusset decreases are completed, the colors will alternate uninterrupted around all needles.

SPECIAL TECHNIQUE

Provisional Cast-On: With crochet hook and waste yarn, make a chain several sts longer than desired cast-on. With knitting needle and project yarn, pick up indicated number of sts in the "bumps" on back of chain. When indicated in pattern, "unzip" the crochet chain to free live sts.

3-Needle Bind-Off: With RS tog and needles parallel, using a third needle, knit a st from the front needle with one from the back. *Knit tog a st from the front and back needles, then slip the first st over the second to bind off. Rep from * across, then fasten off last st.

STITCH PATTERNS

GARTER MOSAIC PATTERN

See Chart.

2-COLOR STRIPE PATTERN

Rnd 1: K1 A, k1 B.
Rnd 2: Knit with A.
Rnd 3: K1 B, k1 B.
Rnd 4: Knit with B.
Rep Rnds 1–4 for color pat.

INSTRUCTIONS

CUFF AND LEG

Using provisional method and A, CO 44 (46) sts.

Row 1 (RS): With A, k8 (10) for garter cuff; beg on Row 5 (1) of chart, work Mosaic pat across next 35 sts, k1.

Row 2 (WS): With A, sl 1 wyif, work Mosaic pat to last 8 (10) sts, k8 (10).

Row 3: With B, sl 1 wyif, k7 (9), work Mosaic pat to last st, k1.

Row 4: With B, sl 1 wyif, work Mosaic pat to last 8 (10) sts, k8 (10).

Continue in this manner, slipping first st of every row until 64 (72) rows of chart have been worked twice. Do not BO.

Unzip the provisional CO and place the live sts on a second dpn.

Holding RS tog, join the live sts using 3-needle BO to form tube.

With B and beg at join of leg, use dpns to pick up and knit 64 (72) sts around leg (one st in each slipped st).

Place first 32 (36) sts onto 1 dpn for heel flap, with rem 32 (36) sts on another dpn for instep sts.

HEEL FLAP

Row 1 (RS): With A, *sl 1, k1; rep from * to end.

Row 2: Sl 1, purl to end.

Rows 3 and 4: With B, rep Rows 1 and 2.

Rep [Rows 1–4] 6 (7) more times—28 (32) rows.

Cut A.

TURN HEEL

Row 1 (RS): With B, k18 (20), ssk, k1; turn.

Row 2: Sl 1, p5, p2tog, p1; turn.

Row 3: Sl 1, knit to 1 st before gap, ssk, k1; turn.

Row 4: Sl 1, purl to 1 st before gap, p2tog, p1; turn.

Rep Rows 3 and 4 until all sts are used up on both sides—18 (20) sts rem.

Next row (RS): K9 (10); join A. This is new beg of rnd.

GUSSET

See Pattern Notes.

Rnd 1 (setup color pat): N1: K1 A, k1 B to end of heel, then, continuing to alternate colors, pick up and knit 14 (16) sts along side of heel; N2: k1 A, k1 B across 32 (36) instep sts; N3: beg with A (B), pick up and knit 14 (16) sts along side of heel, alternating colors of sts, then k9 (10) heel sts continuing in est alternating color pat—78 (88) sts.

Maintaining 2-Color Stripe pat, shape gusset as follows:

Rnd 2: Knit around.

Rnd 3 (dec): N1: Knit to last 3 sts, k2tog, k1; N2: knit across all instep sts; N3: k1, ssk, knit to end—76 (86) sts.

Rep [Rnds 2 and 3] 6 (7) times—64 (72) sts rem, with 16 (18) sts each on N1 and N3 and 32 (36) sts on N2.

FOOT

Work even in est 2-Color Stripe pat until foot measures approx 2 (2½)" [5 (6.5)cm] short of desired length for foot, ending with Rnd 4.

TOE SHAPING

Rnd 1 (dec): With A, work as follows: N1: Knit to last 3 sts, k2tog, k1; N2: k1, ssk, knit to last 3 sts, k2tog, k1; N3: k1, ssk, knit to end—60 (68) sts.

Rnd 2: With B, knit around.

Rep [Rnds 1 and 2] 7 (8) times—32 (36) sts with 8 (9) sts each on N1 and N3 and 16 (18) sts on N2. Cut B.

With A, rep Rnd 1 until 8 sts rem; with N3, k2 from N1, so that there are 4 sts on N2 and N3.

FINISHING

Break yarn, leaving a 10" [25cm] tail.

With tapestry needle and tail, graft toe closed using Kitchener st.

Weave in all ends and block as desired.

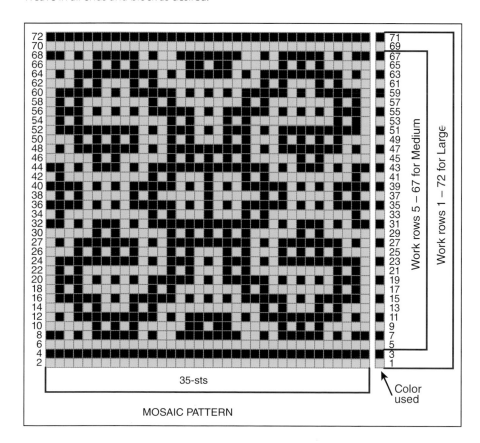

MOSAIC PATTERN

35-sts

Color used

Work rows 5 – 67 for Medium

Work rows 1 – 72 for Large

STITCH AND COLOR KEY

☐ On A rows, knit with A
On B rows, slip with yarn to WS

■ On B rows, knit with B
On A rows, slip with yarn to WS

Notes: Each set of 2 rows (RS/WS) is worked with only 1 color yarn; the colored boxes at the right of the chart indicate the color yarn used on each row.

For WS rows, read the RS row from left-to-right. The sts are worked as they present themselves, i.e. knit the sts that were knit on the RS row and slip the sts that were slipped, holding yarn in front (to WS).

SOUTHERN BELLE SOCKS

DESIGN BY ELIZABETH RAVENWOOD

Southern women are known for being tough and soft, hard-working and elegant, all at the same time. They savor garments that are durable, yet feminine and fashion-forward. For the Southern lady, looking her best, whether while gardening or attending a tea, is essential. This pattern is loosely based on a *Godey's Magazine and Lady's Book* sock pattern. From historical inspiration comes a beautiful, and practical, rendering for today's Southern lady of any age. With enough warmth to make a difference, from one skein of a luxurious blend of wool and silk, these socks continue the elegance of the Southern woman's tradition of sock knitting. ❧

Sizes
Toddler [6–12 months] (child [5–9 years], woman's medium [US size 8–9]).

Instructions are given for smallest size, with larger sizes in parentheses. When only 1 number is given, it applies to all sizes.

Finished Measurements
Circumference: 4½ (6½, 8½)" [11.5 (16.5, 21.5)cm]

Foot length: 4½ (7½, 9)" [11.5 (19, 21.5)cm]

Gauge
40 sts and 60 rnds = 4" [10cm] in St st.

Adjust needle size as necessary to obtain correct gauge.

Materials
- KnitPicks *Gloss Lace* (lace weight; 70% merino wool/30% silk; 440 yds [402m] per 1¾ oz [50g] skein): 1 skein Bare #24178
- Size 0 [2mm] double-pointed needles (set of 5) or size needed to obtain gauge
- Stitch marker
- Tapestry needle

PATTERN NOTES

- This sock is worked from the cuff down, with a heel flap, gusset, and wedge toe.
- Because the lace pattern is very elastic, these socks are easily adjusted for larger or smaller sizes by following the instructions of the size closest to the one you want to make and working the leg and foot shorter or longer, as desired.

SPECIAL ABBREVIATIONS

N1, N2, N3, N4: Needle 1, needle 2, needle 3, needle 4, with heel/sole sts on N1 and N4 and instep sts on N2 and N3.

STITCH PATTERNS

LACE PATTERN (11-ST REP)

Rnd 1: *K1, yo, ssk, yo, ssk, k1, k2tog, yo, k2tog, yo, k1; rep from * around.

Rnds 2, 4, and 6: Knit.

Rnd 3: *K1, yo, ssk, k1, yo, sk2p, yo, k1, k2tog, yo, k1; rep from * around.

Rnd 5: *K1, yo, sk2p, k1, yo, k1, yo, k1, sk2p, yo, k1; rep from * around.

Rnd 7: *K1, yo, sk2p, yo, k3, yo, sk2p, yo, k1; rep from * around.

Rnd 8: Knit.

Rep Rnds 1–8 for pat.

INSTRUCTIONS

CUFF

Using cable cast-on method, CO 44 (66, 78) sts. Divide sts among 4 dpns as follows: 11-11-11-11 (22-11-22-11; 20-20-20-18); mark beg of rnd and join, being careful not to twist the sts.

Work K1, P1 Rib for 10 (20, 20) rnds.

Knit 3 rnds.

Large only

Knit 1 more rnd and dec 12 sts evenly around—66 sts divided on dpns as follows: 22-11-22-11.

LEG

Work 4 (7, 10) reps of 8-rnd Lace pat or until leg measures desired length to ankle, ending with Rnd 8.

HEEL FLAP

Row 1: With 1 dpn, knit across first 2 dpns—22 (33, 33) heel flap sts. Sts on other 2 dpns rem on hold for instep.

Working back and forth on heel sts only, continue as follows:

Row 2 (WS): Sl 1, purl to end.

Row 3: Sl 1, *k1, sl 1; rep from * to last 1 (2, 2) sts, k1 (2, 2).

Rep [Rows 2 and 3] 10 (14, 20) more times—22 (30, 42) rows.

TURN HEEL

Row 1 (WS): Sl 1, p18, p2tog, p1; turn.

Row 2 (RS): Sl 1, k7, ssk, k1; turn.

Row 3: Sl 1, p8, p2tog, p1; turn.

Row 4: Sl 1, k9, ssk, k1; turn.

Cont working in this manner, working 1 more st on each row until all sts have been worked, ending having worked a RS (WS, WS) row—14 (20, 20) sts.

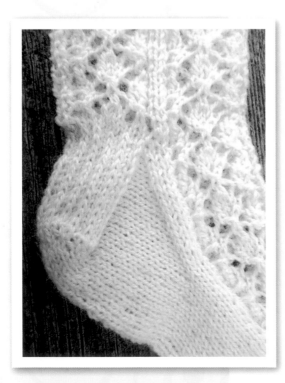

Medium and large only

Knit across heel sts.

GUSSET

Set-up rnd: N1: With RS facing and using dpn holding heel sts, pick up and knit 11 (15, 21) sts along the side of heel flap, then M1 in corner between dpns; N2 and N3 (instep sts): work in est Lace pat across 22 (33, 33) instep sts; N4: M1 in corner between dpns, pick up and knit 11 (15, 21) sts along the second side of heel flap, k7 (10, 10) heel sts from N1—60 (85, 97) sts with 19 (26, 32) sts each on N1 and N4, 11 (22, 22) sts on N2 and 11 sts on N3. Mark beg of rnd at center of sole.

Maintaining sole and gusset sts in St st and instep sts in Lace pat, work as follows:

Rnd 1: Knit.

Rnd 2 (dec): N1: Knit to last 3 sts, k2tog, k1; N2 and N3: work in Lace pat; N4: k1, ssk, knit to end—58 (83, 95) sts.

Rep [Rnds 1 and 2] 7 (9, 15) times—44 (65, 65) sts rem with 11 (16, 16) sts each on N1 and N4 and 22 (33, 33) on N2 and N3.

FOOT

Work even in est pats until foot measures 3½ (6, 7½)" [9.5 (15, 19)cm] from back of heel or approx 1 (1½, 1½)" [2.5 (4, 4)cm] short of desired length, ending having completed Rnd 8 of Lace pat.

TOE

Discontinue Lace pat and work in St st on all sts.

Rnd 1 (dec): N1: *Knit to last 3 sts, k2tog, k1; N2: k1, ssk, knit to end; rep from * on N3 and N4—40 (61, 61) sts.

Rnd 2: Knit.

Rep [Rnds 1 and 2] 4 (10, 9) times—24 (21, 25) sts rem.

Medum and large only

Knit 1 more rnd, working k1, ssk at beg of N2—20 (24) sts.

All sizes

With N4, knit across the sts on N1; transfer sts from N2 to N3. There are now 12 (10, 12) sts on each of 2 dpns. Cut yarn, leaving a 10" [25cm] tail.

With tapestry needle and tail, graft toe closed using Kitchener st.

Weave in all ends. Block.

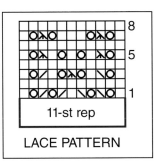

8

5

1

11-st rep

LACE PATTERN

STITCH KEY
☐ Knit
◙ YO
⊠ Ssk
⊠ K2tog
⊠ Sk2p

ANDEAN-INSPIRED SOCKS

DESIGN BY GRETCHEN FUNK

The knitting tradition of the people of the Andes Mountains is highly revered around the world. The region is perhaps best known for its chul'la hats, characterized by either a riot of color or simpler patterns in more subdued, earthy tones. These cozy socks, inspired by the colorful designs found on the pages of *Andean Folk Knits*, by Marcia Lewandowski, combine a bright colorway on a more subdued, neutral ground. The drawstring at the top of the sock was modeled on the small colorful drawstring purses featured in the book. ❧

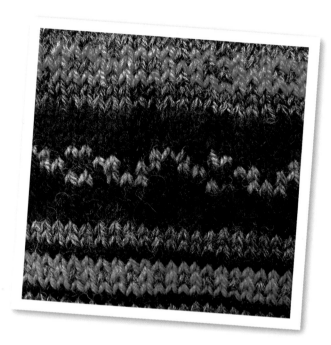

Sizes

Woman's small [US size 6–8] (medium [US size 8–10], large [US size 9–12]). Instructions are given for the smallest size, with larger sizes in parentheses. When only one number is given, it applies to all sizes.

Finished Measurements

Length from cuff to ankle: 9 (10, 11)" [23 (25.5, 28)cm]

Circumference: 8 (8½, 9)" [20.5 (21.5, 23)cm]

Materials 🔢2

- Brown Sheep *Nature Spun Sport Weight* (sport weight; 100% wool; 184 yds [168m] per 1¾ oz [50g] skein): 2 (3, 3) skeins Stone #701 (A); 1 skein each Storm #114 (B), Burnt Sienna #101 (C), Sunburst Gold #308 (D), Ash #720 (E), and Meadow Green #N56 (F)

- Size 1 [2.25mm] needles for I-cord

- Size 3 [3mm] double-pointed needles (set of 4) or a 40" [100cm] circular (for magic loop) or size to obtain gauge

- Size 4 [3.5mm] double-pointed needles (set of 4) or a 40" [100cm] circular (for magic loop) or size needed to obtain gauge for colorwork

- Stitch marker

- Tapestry needle

Gauge

26 sts and 37 rnds = 4" [10cm] in St st using smaller needles and 2-color stranded St st using larger needles.

Adjust needle size as necessary to obtain correct gauge.

PATTERN NOTES

- ◆ This sock is worked from the cuff down with a heel flap, gusset, and wedge toe.
- ◆ 2-color stranded stockinette stitch tends to pull in more than 1-color stockinette stitch, so work color pattern with a larger set of needles to obtain gauge.
- ◆ Slipped stitches are slipped purlwise unless specified as being slipped knitwise. Stitches on the heel flap are twisted by slipping them knitwise, thereby creating a denser fabric.
- ◆ If using suggested yarn, gently hand-wash the socks to prevent felting.

INSTRUCTIONS

CUFF

With largest dpns and A, CO 52 (56, 60) sts.

Distribute sts evenly on 3 mid-size dpns; mark beg of rnd and join, being careful not to twist sts.

Rnds 1–4: Work K2, P2 Rib around.

Rnd 5: K2 (0, 2), p2 (0, 2), *k2, yo, p2tog; rep from * around.

Rnds 6-9: Work K2, P2 Rib around.

LEG

Next rnd: Change to largest dpns; knit and dec 2 (inc 4, --) sts evenly around—50 (60, 60) sts.

Knit 4 rnds.

Work 28 rnds following Chart.

Next rnd: Change to mid-size dpns; knit and inc 2 (dec 4, --) sts evenly around—52 (56, 60) sts.

With A, knit until leg measures 3½ (4, 4½)" [9 (10, 11.5)cm] from last colorwork rnd.

HEEL FLAP

Row 1 (RS): With 1 dpn and B, knit across first 16 (14, 18) sts, turn.

Row 2: Sl 1, purl across first 25 (27, 30) sts, turn. Sts on this needle are heel flap sts; redistribute rem 26 (28, 30) sts on 2 dpns and keep on hold for instep.

Row 3: Sl 1, *k1, sl 1 kwise; rep from * to last st, k1.

Row 4: Sl 1, purl to end.

Rep [Rows 1 and 2] 11 (12, 13) more times. Cut B.

TURN HEEL

Row 1 (RS): Change to A; sl 1, k14 (16, 18) ssk, k1, turn.

Row 2 (WS): Sl 1, p5 (7, 9), p2tog, p1, turn.

Row 3: Sl 1, k6 (8, 10) ssk, k1, turn.

Row 4: Sl 1, p7 (9, 11), p2tog, p1, turn

Cont working in this manner, working 1 more st on each row until all sts have been worked, ending with a WS row—16 (18, 20) sts

GUSSET

Pick-up rnd: N1: Knit across heel sts, then pick up and knit 13 (14, 15) sts along the left edge of heel flap; N2: knit across instep sts; N3: pick up and knit 13 (14, 15) sts along the right edge of heel, k8 (9, 10) sts to center of heel—68 (74, 80) sts with 21 (23, 25) sts on N1 and N3 and 26 (28, 30) sts on N2.

Rnd 1: N1: Knit to last 3 sts, k2tog, k1; N2: knit; N3: k1, ssk, knit to end—66 (72, 78) sts.

Rnd 2: Knit around.

Rep [Rnds 1 and 2] 7 (8, 9) more times—52 (56, 60) sts, with 13 (14, 15) sts on N1 and N3.

FOOT

Work even until foot measures 8 (9, 10)" [20.5 (23, 25.5)cm] from back of heel or 2" (2¼, 2½)" [5 (5.5, 6.5)cm] short of desired length. Cut A.

TOE

Rnd 1 (dec): N1: With B, knit to last 3 sts, k2tog, k1; N2: k1, ssk, knit to last 3 sts, k2tog, k1; N3: k1, ssk, knit to end—48 (52, 56) sts.

Rnd 2: Knit around.

Rep [Rnds 1 and 2] 9 (10, 11) times—12 sts rem.

Cut yarn, leaving a 12" [30.5cm] tail.

With tapestry needle and tail, graft toe closed using Kitchener st.

FINISHING

Weave in all ends. Block socks.

I-Cord

With B and smallest dpns, CO 3 sts, leaving a 10" [25.5cm] tail.

*K3, do not turn, slip sts back to LH needle; rep from * until cord measures approx 20" [51cm]. Bind off.

Pull I-cord through the eyelets so the ends are at the center back of sock and covering the gap in the eyelets on small and large sizes.

Tassels

With several colors of project yarn, make 2 tassels about 2" [5cm] long. Secure to ends of I-cord.

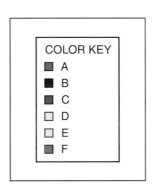

COLOR KEY
- A
- B
- C
- D
- E
- F

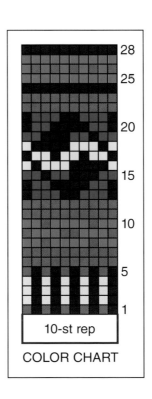

10-st rep

COLOR CHART

ABBREVIATIONS

beg	begin, beginning, begins
BO	bind off
CC	contrast color
cm	centimeter(s)
CO	cast on
cont	continue, continuing
dec(s)	decrease, decreasing, decreases
dpn	double-pointed needle(s)
est	establish, established
foll	follow(s), following
inc(s)	increase(s), increasing
k	knit
k1f&b	knit into front then back of same st (increase)
k1f,b,&f	knitting into front, back, then front again of same st (increase 2 sts)
k1-tbl	knit 1 st through back loop
k2tog	knit 2 sts together (decrease)
k2tog-tbl	knit 2 sts together through back loops
kwise	knitwise (as if to knit)
LH	left-hand
m(s)	marker(s)
MC	main color
mm	millimeter(s)
M1	make 1 (increase)
M1k	make 1 knitwise
M1p	make 1 purlwise
pat(s)	pattern(s)
p	purl
p1f&b	purl into front then back of same st (increase)
p1-tbl	purl 1 st through back loop
p2tog	purl 2 sts together (decrease)
pm	place marker

psso	pass slip st(s) over
pwise	purlwise (as if to purl)
rem	remain(s), remaining
rep(s)	repeat(s), repeated, repeating
rnd(s)	round(s)
RH	right-hand
RS	right side (of work)
rev sc	reverse single crochet (crab st)
sc	single crochet
sl	slip, slipped, slipping
ssk	[slip 1 st knitwise] twice from left needle to right needle, insert left needle tip into fronts of both slipped sts, knit both sts together from this position (decrease)
ssp	[slip 1 st knitwise] twice from left needle to right needle, return both sts to left needle and purl both together through back loops
st(s)	stitch(es)
St st	stockinette stitch
tbl	through back loop
tog	together
W&T	wrap next stitch then turn work (often used in short rows)
WS	wrong side (of work)
wyib	with yarn in back
wyif	with yarn in front
yb	yarn back
yf	yarn forward
yo	yarn over
*	repeat instructions from *
( )	alternate measurements and/or instructions
[ ]	instructions to be worked as a group a specified number of times

YARN SOURCES

Alpaca with a Twist
www.alpacawithatwist.com

Blue Moon Fiber Arts
www.bluemoonfiberarts.com

Brown Sheep
www.brownsheep.com

Cascade Yarns
www.cascadeyarns.com

Dream in Color
www.dreamincoloryarn.com

Elemental Affects
www.elementalaffects.com

Frangipani
www.guernseywool.co.uk

Helmi Vuorelma Oy
www.kauppa.vourelma.net

Ístex
www.istex.is

Jamieson's
www.jamiesonshetland.co.uk

KnitPicks
www.knitpicks.com

Lana Grossa
www.lanagrossa.com

Loop-d-Loop
Distributed by Tahki Stacy Charles Inc.
www.tahkistacycharles.com

Lorna's Laces
www.lornaslaces.net

The March Hare
www.etsy.com/shop/MegWarren

Mission Falls
www.missionfalls.com

Reynold's
www.jcacrafts.com

Saga Hill Designs
www.sagahill.com

Shalimar Yarns
www.shalimaryarns.com

Shibuiknits
www.shibuiknits.com

Wendy Knits
http://wendyknits.net/

STANDARD YARN WEIGHT SYSTEM

Categories of yarn, gauge ranges, and recommended needle and hook sizes

Yarn Weight Symbol & Category Names	0 Lace	1 Super Fine	2 Fine	3 Light	4 Medium	5 Bulky	6 Super Bulky
Type of Yarns in Category	Fingering 10 count crochet thread	Sock, Fingering, Baby	Sport, Baby	DK, Light Worsted	Worsted, Afghan, Aran	Chunky, Craft, Rug	Bulky, Roving
Knit Gauge Range* in Stockinette Stitch to 4 inches	33–40** sts	27–32 sts	23–26 sts	21–24 sts	16–20 sts	12–15 sts	6–11 sts
Recommended Needle in Metric Size Range	1.5–2.25 mm	2.25–3.25 mm	3.25–3.75 mm	3.75–4.5 mm	4.5–5.5 mm	5.5–8 mm	8 mm and larger
Recommended Needle U.S. Size Range	000 to 1	1 to 3	3 to 5	5 to 7	7 to 9	9 to 11	11 and larger
Crochet Gauge* Ranges in Single Crochet to 4 inch	32–42 double crochets**	21–32 sts	16–20 sts	12–17 sts	11–14 sts	8–11 sts	5–9 sts
Recommended Hook in Metric Size Range	Steel*** 1.6–1.4mm Regular hook 2.25 mm	2.25–3.5 mm	3.5–4.5 mm	4.5–5.5 mm	5.5–6.5 mm	6.5–9 mm	9 mm and larger
Recommended Hook U.S. Size Range	Steel*** 6, 7, 8 Regular hook B–1	B–1 to E–4	E–4 to 7	7 to I–9	I–9 to K–10½	K–10½ to M–13	M–13 and larger

* GUIDELINES ONLY: The above reflect the most commonly used gauges and needle or hook sizes for specific yarn categories.

** Lace weight yarns are usually knitted or crocheted on larger needles and hooks to create lacy, openwork patterns. Accordingly, a gauge range is difficult to determine. Always follow the gauge stated in your pattern.

*** Steel crochet hooks are sized differently from regular hooks--the higher the number, the smaller the hook, which is the reverse of regular hook sizing.

This Standards & Guidelines booklet and downloadable symbol artwork are available at: **YarnStandards.com**

ABOUT THE DESIGNERS

Star Athena has a degree in art (painting and printmaking) and has played around with many crafts. Star's grandma taught her to knit when she was around nine, and she grows more addicted every year. She loves how knitting combines creativity with practicality. Working in yarn shops has given Star opportunities to interact with a wider knitting community. In Portland, Oregon, where she lives, Star's favorite yarn haunt is Twisted. Star admits that she's not entirely monogamous with knitting, as she likes to explore other fiberarts such as crochet and spinning. When she's not crafting, Star likes to listen to records, read, play games, eat chocolate, solve puzzles, and explore the Pacific Northwest.

Dawn Brocco began her designing career working freelance for most of the major knitting publications. She has been self-publishing for the past thirteen years, and now has over a hundred patterns available. Her style embraces classic design with modern twists, and whimsical design based on a love of nature. You can find Dawn Brocco Knitwear Designs at www.dawnbrocco.com and you can reach Dawn at dawn@dawnbrocco.com.

Beth Brown-Reinsel has been teaching knitting workshops nationally, as well as internationally, for more than twenty years. She wrote the book *Knitting Ganseys* and has recently filmed the DVD *Knitting Ganseys with Beth Brown-Reinsel*. Her articles have appeared in *Threads; Cast On; Interweave Knits; Shuttle, Spindle, and Dye Pot; Vogue Knitting*, and *Knitters* magazines. She continues to design for her own pattern line, available at www.knittingtraditions.com. Beth lives happily in Vermont.

Nancy Bush found her way to traditional knitting techniques and uses of ethnic patterns via a degree in art history and post–graduate studies in color design and weaving in San Francisco and Sweden. She has published articles and designs in *Knitter's, Interweave Knits, Vogue Knitting,* and *Threads*. She has been the knitting contributor to *PieceWork* magazine and is currently a member of the editorial advisory panel. She teaches workshops in the United States and abroad. She is the author of *Folk Socks* (1994), *Folk Knitting in Estonia* (1999), *Knitting on the Road: Socks for the Traveling Knitter* (2001), *Knitting Vintage Socks* (2005), and *Knitted Lace of Estonia: Techniques, Patterns, and Traditions* (2008), all published by Interweave Press. She owns the Wooly West, a mail-order yarn business in Salt Lake City, Utah.

Tatyana Chambers was born and raised in Russia, where she lived in the ancient city of Astrakhan on the Volga River. Tatyana learned to knit from a neighbor when she was in fourth grade, and she has been knitting on and off ever since. Later she taught herself to crochet and felt, and she began designing her own accessories using a variety of knitting and felting techniques. Tatyana studied art and worked as a graphic designer until 2004, when she moved to the United States. Tatyana now lives in Alexandria, Virginia, where she runs her own business, Wool Thumb Creations, designing hand-crafted accessories made from wool for women and home. You can find Tatyana's designs on www.etsy.com.

Donna Druchunas is the author of numerous books, including *Successful Lace Knitting: Celebrating the Work of Dorothy Reade, Ethnic Knitting Exploration: Lithuania, Iceland, and Ireland,* and *Arctic Lace: Knitted Projects and Stories Inspired by Alaska's Native Knitters*. She spent four months this year traveling in Europe to teach knitting workshops and do research for her next book, which will be about knitting in Lithuania. Visit her website at www.sheeptoshawl.com.

Teva Durham grew up in St. Louis, Missouri, with rather unconventional parents who met in art school. As a teenager, Teva moved to New York City, attended the High School of Performing Arts, and collected vintage clothing for costumes. Teva developed a particular fondness for sweaters culled from Lower Manhattan thrift shops and soon took up knitting. After pursuing acting and journalism, Teva made a career out of her obsessive hobby and launched one of the first online knitting pattern sites, www.loop-d-loop.com, in 2000. She is the author of *Loop-d-Loop* (STC Craft 2005) and *Loop-d-Loop Crochet* (STC Craft 2007) and produces a line of yarns distributed by Tahki Stacy Charles.

Gretchen Funk lives and knits in Minnesota, where she and her husband own and operate the Triple Rock Social Club. She teaches knitting at the Yarnery in St. Paul and Crafty Planet, a needlework and craft shop in Minneapolis.

Chrissy Gardiner is a knitwear designer and teacher living in Portland, Oregon. She is the author of *Toe-Up! Patterns and Worksheets to Whip Your Sock Knitting into Shape* and the upcoming *Indie Socks*. She has also contributed designs to numerous books and magazines, and published her own pattern line. You can see more of her work at www.gardineryarnworks.com.

Anne Carrol Gilmour owned and operated Wildwest Woolies, a full-spectrum textile arts shop in Evanston, Wyoming, for nearly six years. She now lives in the beautiful Wasatch Mountains near Park City, Utah, where she works in her studio and also teaches workshops in spinning, weaving, and knitting. Her work has been featured in various textile publications and many galleries, museums, and private collections worldwide. A first-generation American, she readily admits that her Celtic roots show up frequently in her designs. When not elbow-deep in wool, Anne enjoys her family, pets, the great outdoors, reading, music, and dancing. Many of her knitwear patterns are also available on her website: www.wildwestwoolies.com.

Three years ago, **Elanor Lynn** relocated from Brooklyn, New York, to Hollywood, California. Since then, she's been knitting lots of palm trees into tapestries. She's currently exploring "handwritten" fonts in text-based work.

Wendy J. Johnson is a fiber artist, teacher, photographer, author, and graphic artist specializing in design legibility. She has been knitting, weaving, dyeing, and spinning for more than thirty years and has taught fiber arts for more than ten years. Her first experience with needles and yarn came from her Swedish grandmotherm who knit every night at the kitchen table. Wendy's Swedish heritage continues to have a strong influence in her design work. Along with her creative arts business, Saga Hill Designs, Wendy is a consultant on aging vision through her legibility firm, www.ElderEye.com. Today, Wendy spins and knits at the same kitchen table she shared with her grandmother—now located in Orono, Minnesota. She can be contacted at www.sagahill.com.

Janel Laidman has been obsessed with knitting since 1980, when she discovered that Danish girls could knit socks and learn physics at the same time. In the quest to reach the same lofty heights of coolness, she taught herself to knit too. Today Janel spends her time designing socks and other knitted garments, writing knitting books, feeding tulips to the deer, and knitting of course! Janel is the author of *The Enchanted Sole: Legendary Socks for Adventurous Knitters*.

Hélène Magnússon is best known for her research on the traditional intarsia seen in knitted inserts in Icelandic shoes for centuries. Her book, *Icelandic Knitting: Using Rose Patterns*, is available In three languages. She Is a French native, but a true Icelandic knitter with an Icelandic family. Hélène abandoned a law career in Paris for the love of the Icelandic outdoors. She worked as a mountain guide for many years in Iceland and studied textile design at the Iceland Academy of the Arts. Find out more about her on her website, www.helenemagnusson.com

A native of Ohio, **Annie Modesitt** taught herself to knit at the age of twenty-five, before a move from New York City to Texas. The Texas tenure didn't last, but knitting did, and upon her return to the New York area, Annie began knitting for other designers and designing for major knitting magazines. Her work has appeared in *Interweave Knits, Vogue Knitting, Knitters Magazine, Cast On, Family Circle Easy Knitting, McCalls Needlework*, and several family-oriented magazines. Find out more on her website, www.anniemodesitt.com.

Heather Ordover, an award-winning New York City high-school teacher, transitioned into writing full time after ten years in the classroom. Ordover has written and recorded essays for *Cast-On: A Podcast for Knitters* and currently hosts her own long-running

podcast, *CraftLit: A Podcast for Crafters Who Love Books* (think "books on tape with benefits"). Her crafty writing has appeared in *Spin-Off, WeaveZine*, and *The Arizona Daily Star*. She currently teaches writing in Tucson, Arizona, where she lives with her amused husband, two goofy sons, their devoted dogs, and a single, mournful blue-tongued skink. Oh, and she knits.

Beth Parrott Beth Parrott has been knitting for more than 60 years. She is the co-author of *The Little Box of Socks* and *Sock Club* with Charlen Schurch, both published by Martingale & Company. Beth lives and knits in Charleston, South Carolina.

Elizabeth Ravenwood knits, crochets, spins, writes, and creates in the Deep South. Always testing the boundaries of what can be done in a creative life, she writes articles and books sharing her knowledge and creative adventures. Elizabeth lives in Georgia with four dogs, six cats, and a house full of puppet people.

Kristin Spurkland learned to knit from her roommate, Sophie, in her freshman year of college. In 1998, she received her degree in apparel design from Bassist College in Portland, Oregon, and decided to pursue a career in knitwear design. She has been designing ever since. Kristin is the author of four books, including *The Knitting Man(ual)* (Ten Speed Press, 2007).

Candace Eisner Strick has immersed herself in music and knitting most of her life. Now retired from sixteen years of teaching cello, she concentrates on desiging, writing, and teaching knitting. Her newest book, *Strick-ly Socks*, features a revolutionary and amazingly simple way of knitting socks. She is the author of six other books, has been published in numerous magazines, and has taught nationally and internationally since 1998. She is the creator of her own line of yarn, Merging Colors, and her own line of patterns under the name of Strickwear. (www.strickwear.com). You can read her blog at http://candaceeisnerstrickknitting.blogspot.com/.

Pinpilan Wangsai was a massive failure when her grade-school teacher tried to teach her to crochet. After almost ten years of firmly believing she would never be able to make anything from yarn except pom poms, she tried again in college. Something clicked, and she went on to teach herself to knit almost anything by looking at books, Internet pages, and asking kind knitterly friends. She is now working as an elementary school teacher by day and knitting, spinning, or dreaming up new things by night.

Anna Zilboorg took her love of yarn and knitting around the world and into the hills. The result has been countless knitting designs published in various magazines and a number of books, two of which feature sock designs: *Socks for Sandals and Clogs* and *Magnificent Mittens and Socks*. Anna is also the author of *Knitting for Anarchists*, a must-read for understanding how stitches are formed.

INDEX